REPOSITORY

REPOSITORY

REPOSITORY

49 Methods and Assignments for Writing Urban Places

edited by
Carlos Machado e Moura, Dalia Milián Bernal,
Esteban Restrepo Restrepo, Klaske Havik, Lorin Niculae

nai010publishers

Introduction

REPOSITORY
49 Methods and Assignments for Writing Urban Places

Carlos Machado e Moura, Dalia Milián Bernal,
Esteban Restrepo Restrepo, Klaske Havik, Lorin Niculae

Jorge Luis Borges's short story *The Library of Babel* (1944) presents us with an endless structure, a sequence of hexagonal rooms beyond sight with an almost infinite number of books. In a small footnote, the narrator points out that *"In order for a book to exist, it is sufficient that it be possible. Only the impossible is excluded. For example, no book is also a staircase, though there are no doubt books that discuss and deny and prove that possibility, and others whose structure corresponds to that of a staircase"*.[1] What we present here however, tries to achieve what for Borges was impossible: to make a book (also) be a building, a container, a repository. But it also attempts to provide a device that, beyond collecting, is actually a generator of new content.

Unlike an inventory or catalogue, which comprise an itemized, arranged enumeration of elements ordered systematically, this Repository is more than a container where something is simply deposited or stored; it assumes the form of a book. Nevertheless, to be fair with the process of its own construction, we should say that this is a Repository that gradually adopted the form of a book, without losing its architectural attributes. In fact, this Repository was first built in a virtual interactive environment, where its content has been in permanent expansion, discussion, and auto-generation. In this, we take inspiration from the impossible work which Stéphane Mallarmé undertook during the last thirty years of his life, trying to build an 'absolute book' that would condense the whole essence of his literature and reality. Simply called *Le Livre* (1898), it was made of a series of unbound pamphlets, loose sheets with no predefined reading order, allowing every possible combination.

The Repository, as much as Borges' *Library* and Mallarmé's *Livre*, is an attempt to build a hypertext, a flexible, interactive, open work, offering a kaleidoscopic and non-sequential reading. Rather than trying to understand the world, the ultimate function of this Repository would be to produce encounters and autonomous forms that could be added to those already existing. As such, the aim of this Repository joins the challenge of preserving the openness and multiplicity of dimensions and agents present in the rich array of methods that compose it.

Towards a Repository...

This Repository gathers a series of methods and assignments born from a shared interest in urban narratives. What can narratives tell us about how communities relate to place? How can existing stories of place allow us to write new narratives for the city? How can we read the stories that are inscribed in streets, on walls, and in architectural details? How can archives unveil hidden stories of places and buildings, and of their makers and users? How can we write the city by using our senses? This Repository can be seen as an invitation, encouraging scholars, students, and spatial practitioners to explore 49 methods, and, through clearly laid out assignments, take them out into the field.

This Repository is the result of over three years of intense collaboration within the framework of the European COST Action, *Writing Urban Places*, a diverse group of scholars in the fields of architecture, urban studies, literature, sociology and other disciplines interested in the value of local urban narratives – stories rich in information regarding citizens' socio-spatial practices, perceptions and expectations.[2] Working Group 3 of this network was dedicated to the articulation of concrete devices to unveil, study, and write urban narratives and to explore their potential for strategies of design, to generate new (and counter) narratives, and to reveal subjugated voices.

The group shared knowledge and experience about the methods they use to find, interpret and even produce urban narratives. A long process of dialogue took place within the group, first by collecting and discussing descriptions of methods on Padlet, an online platform where ideas can be shared. Through this digital instrument, participants were able to analyse the methods shared by similarities, objectives and output, fields and disciplines involved, procedures in data collection, place and, last but not least, the techniques and procedures used, thus fostering international research partnerships.

The next step in the process was clarifying the methods, bringing the descriptions down to the basic elements of each method, in order to increase the communicability of the method in a very concise way. This process of distilling a sometimes-broad description of a method to only one page was one of the greatest synthesising efforts on the part of the authors of this publication. Furthermore, from the descriptive level, we searched for a format to activate the methods, discussing their practical use in fieldwork. Therefore, we asked the participants to articulate assignments that might formulate specific responses, potentially becoming case studies for the application of the method.

In April 2021, the group organised the online webinar, "Reading, Writing and Activating Urban Places," a mini-conference which brought together a large number of topics. The contributions were presented in a dynamic way, using a PechaKucha format, where researchers presented their methods with 20 slides, each slide being shown for 20 seconds only. The 3 panels of the webinar, which delineated three main categories of methods used to understanding the city – transcribing it with words into sentences and transforming it by design – were followed by reflections and discussions that detailed and enriched the presentations.[3]

This Repository thus came to fruition thanks to an intense collective effort bringing together almost as many different voices as the set of methods it gathers. We do not take this effort for granted. As we were planning this project, unimaginably, most cities across the globe put into place social distancing measures and urban populations were ordered into lockdown due to the covid-19 pandemic. For some of us, this project became a form of togetherness at a time of profound isolation. Unable to leave our homes and affected by our local realities, our ways of engaging with each other and urban places inevitably changed. For many, interaction with the city became possible only through window views, and discussions about urban life in locked-down cities were only feasible in online venues.

It is within this context that new, creative, and humane approaches to engaging, researching, understanding, planning, and creating urban places find renewed importance. While this unprecedented situation catalysed novel forms of solidarities and creative, collective urban experiences, it also exacerbated socio-spatial inequalities and injustices and visualised their pervasiveness in urban places. During the work on this Repository, we realised that *another* way to interact with urban places is not only possible but necessary. A disassociated form of urban inquiry is no longer viable and the construction of segregating or even alienating urban environments based on dispossession and the destruction of nature must cease to be the norm. This Repository is a call for action and an invitation to interact with material and immaterial dimensions of urban places in a more caring, compassionate, collective way and with all our senses activated.

...of Methods and Assignments...

According to the Merriam-Webster dictionary, a method can be defined as "a way, technique, or process of or for doing something".[4] The word derives from the Ancient Greek *méthodos* from *meta* "in pursuit or quest of," and, *hodos*, "a way or manner," and "a travelling, motion, journey... a path, track, road".[5] The methods collected here can indeed be seen as particular ways to approach urban sites, and the assignments as steps to take along these 'ways'. The assignments are systematic procedures of acting that offer ways to explore, examine and discover urban places. In this repository, all methods are entitled by means of verbs, rather than nouns, indicating that we see these methods as active engagements with the city.

However, methods do not emerge in a vacuum; they are underpinned by different ontological and epistemological positions and assumptions. The ways we choose to inquire about the world around us are strongly influenced by who we are and where we stand. The choice for the use of particular methods thus inevitably has a political dimension. And when it comes down to the politics of *methods and the city*, a critical reference to the Chicago School is inevitable.

The Chicago School was established in the late 1800s at a moment of rapid urban growth and at a time in which *the city* started to receive scholarly attention. Particularly the city of Chicago – which some argue emerged at the time as an "instant metropolis" (Lutters & Ackerman, 1996) – attracted an interdisciplinary group of scholars for whom the city became, "at once, the object and the venue of study" (Gieryn, 2006). These scholars viewed (and treated) the city as a field-site and, as such, the tools, approaches, and methods used by anthropologists to study *others elsewhere* were adopted and adapted for the purpose of studying *the city* and its emerging urban society – being particularly attentive to the "social problems of the day" (Hunter, 1980). Paradoxically, they also adopted and adapted the rhetoric of the natural sciences referring to *the city* as "a social laboratory". Their accounts and representations of the city are frequently described as ecological and evolutionist. However, their approach to "the city as a social laboratory," is far more than mere rhetoric; it epitomises an epistemic assumption that researchers can study the social world entirely outside and disassociated from it – like in a laboratory.

This assumption, not yet fully overcome, is particularly problematic for at least two reasons. First, it presupposes a certain higher positionality of the researcher in relation to the city and its society. Secondly, as these scholars "purposely focused upon disorganisation precisely because [their research] was oriented to [...] social reform," (Hunter, 1980) their scholarly work had a direct impact on urban reform, policy, and built environments well beyond Chicago (Baeten, 2017) and rarely for the advancement of social justice. So, while the Chicago School marked an important referent in urban studies; "its scholars left behind an abundance of research monographs and manuals in research methods" (Gieryn, 2006 p. 7); it produced some of the most intriguing maps of the city of Chicago[6]; are renowned for their highly qualitative research approach and praised for their rigorous data collection methods (Lutters & Ackerman, 1996); their story is also a reminder of the political dimension (and power) of methods and narratives.

Nevertheless, these narratives and approaches have not gone unchallenged and, since then, an array of critical epistemological and theoretical perspectives have emerged, from Marxists in the 1960s and 1970s in North-Western Europe and post-socialist perspectives in Eastern Europe to decolonial movements all over the world. Amongst others, feminists have (in their activist and scholarly constellations) fervently contested the belief in an objective (thus, dissociated) form of social enquiry and questioned the role and position of the researcher – the subject of knowledge (Tuana, 2017). Feminist epistemology argues that knowledge and its generation are subjective and situated, never value-free and always contextual. The contestation of the position of the subject of knowledge has also been the point of departure of subaltern studies in Europe, South-East Asia (precursor to postcolonial theory), and Latin America (precursor to decolonial thinking).

In Europe, critical urban theory, in the Marxist tradition (through Henri Lefebvre), emerges directly as an antagonist to the approaches of the Chicago School, emphasising "the politically and ideologically mediated, socially contested and therefore malleable character of urban space" (Brenner, 2009, p. 198). These critical urban thinkers are not alone and have certainly influenced the uprising of dissident perspectives from the Global South, including postcolonial urban theorists such as Ananya Roy (2016) and anarchist urban theorists, like Marcelo López de Souza (2012), who are also influencing urban scholarly work in the Global North.

Furthermore, these emerging and always evolving critical perspectives have also opened up the possibility of multiple, novel, and creative ways to critique capitalism's 'modes and relations of production' (Lefebvre, 1991) while simultaneously pursuing knowledge about urban places. By doing so, they brought subjugated voices, stories, and narratives to the fore, and revealed new venues from which knowledge and theoretical insights could be drawn. All of these dimensions are particularly visible in the subversive approaches adopted by the politically-engaged and art-driven group, Situationist International, whose legacy remains relevant today and is latent in several contributions in this Repository.

This Repository celebrates this proliferation, multiplicity and cohabitation of thoughts and visions and thus gathers, not the most fixed, mainstream and institutionalised methods to read, perform, or write urban places, but a series of innovative and creative procedures deriving from different horizons in order to expose the diversity in which the city might be grasped, told, and expressed and thereby also produced. It intends to stimulate new approaches in architecture, urban studies, and other fields of spatial development and to invite creative, often embodied, and sometimes playful engagements with the material and immaterial dimensions of urban places.

…for Writing Urban Places.

The multiple entries of this Repository reveal methods with different purposes, themes, media, and formats. Some are predominantly oriented to data collection, surveying or understanding reality through the identification of the elements that define a given environment with qualitative and quantitative types of research. It is the case of *Localizing Details; Building Consensus on Place Representation; Charting People, Activities and Places*; or *Streaming the Urban*. Others aim deliberately at transforming that place, interpreting its characteristics by means of activation, either through design operations, like in *Designing by Participation with Giancarlo de Carlo*, or via more activist approaches, as in *Co-Creating,* and in, *Intervening Tactically*.

The marks of memories from the past, the tangible or invisible structures of power, the shared qualities of a community, or the presence of nature, compose the large and diverse array of themes they address. Dealing with these different approaches and agendas, inevitably requires different tools. Our body might be the principal instrument in perceiving or transforming reality in embodied approaches, like *Bordering, Tailoring Ethnography* and *Performing (on) Architecture with Theatre Protocols*; or the walking-based methods of *Aimless wandering, Horizontal viewing*, and *Walking backwards*. Others are mediated in their outputs, as is the case of the visual methods, which operate with drawing or photography, such as: *Revisiting postcards* or *Double-exposing Place*; as well as with text-based methods like: *Writing at 1:50; Making Material Sense; Uncannying the Ordinary… with Cortázar;* or *Exhausting Urban Places à la Georges Perec*. Equally mediated are those which generate diagrams to synthesise information such as: *Walking and Scoring*, or *Surveying with the PlaceMaker Method*; or even generate maps, namely when creating pedestrian routes such as in: *Planning and Walking Thematic Routes* and *Mapping Graffiti and Street Art*; or in the application of graph theory in *Connecting the Nodes*. Other methods incorporate the possibilities promised by artificial intelligence or those already offered by virtual space – such as *Geotagging the Urban Landscape* or *Performing the City from Cyberspace*.

Combinations are also frequent, either merging visual and text-based methods like the visual urban essays of *Framing the City in Words and Images*, or the mix of performative and image-based approaches in *Weaving Stories*, or *Re-acting with Images*. Another type of combination relates to transactions and interactions between the objects of analysis, either between buildings (as in *Appraising*), between the city and characters (*Transcribing the City as Character*), or between human and non-human beings (*Imagining Dialogues with the Voiceless,* or *Playing City-making*). Some methods, however, are mediated not only in their outputs but also in their objects, because rather than dealing directly with reality, they work with their registers or representations – either by looking at literary texts, as with *Reading the City*; by delving into the archives, as in *Re-activating Minor Matters of Archival Documents*, and *Assembling Pasts*; by performing a rhetorical analysis of all sorts of media in *Recapturing the City*, or by combining the physical experience of space with archival research, as in *Stacking Narratives*.

Each method is translated into practical assignments that are meant to take different durations, from hours or one day, like *Scaling Stories*, or *Transforming through Active Space*, to several days or longer periods – as in *Atlasing Urban Experience* or *Meaning-making*. According to their structure, some assignments are also ready to be implemented individually, such as *(multi)Styling Places… with Queneau; Site-writing; Storying Stories*; or *Eavesdropping*, while other are more suitable to be performed collectively in a group, eventually in workshops, as in *Drawing collectively; Engaging (with) Images*; or *Collaging Community Narratives*.

We want this Repository to be a practical tool, an open document, and a living device. In it, each method is described in a short text and is accompanied by an assignment. The assignments are a central element of this Repository, as they interpret, complete, or continue the methods themselves, but also encourage a constant dialogue between contributors and users, through a series of experiments and practices within the urban space. Each assignment is presented as a clear set of numbered instructions to guide the reader to explore and employ the method.

As such, this Repository is intended to stay off the shelves and aims to be a useful tool to inspire, accompany, and assist spatial professionals, researchers, students, and non-academic communities alike to engage with urban places and to discover and develop responsible approaches to current urban challenges.

1 Borges, J.L. (1944). The Library of Babel. In *Collected Fictions*. Trans. Andrew Hurley. New York: Penguin, 1998, 117
2 The EU COST Action network *Writing Urban Places: New Narratives of the European City* is an interdisciplinary group of international scholars. The Action Writing Urban Places focuses on the potential of narrative methods for urban development in European medium-sized cities. https://writingurbanplaces.eu
3 Some of these contributions further developed into full-fledged academic articles, which after a process of peer review were published in 2021 in the *Writingplace Journal* issue #5 "Narrative Methods for Writing Urban Places. https://journals.open.tudelft.nl/writingplace/issue/view/878
4 Method. In *Merriam-Webster.com dictionary*. Retrieved November 25, 2022, from https://www.merriam-webster.com/dictionary/method
5 Method. In *Etymonline.com Online Etymology Dictionary*. Retrieved November 25, 2022, from https://www.etymonline.com/search?q=method
6 *Mapping Chicago - Mapping the Young Metropolis - The University of Chicago Library*. (n.d.). Retrieved November 25, 2022, from https://www.lib.uchicago.edu/collex/exhibits/mapping-young-metropolis/mapping-chicago.

References

Baeten, G. (2017). Neoliberal planning. In *The Routledge handbook of planning theory* (105-117). Routledge.

Borges, J.L. (1944). The Library of Babel. In *Collected Fictions*. Trans. Andrew Hurley. New York: Penguin, 1998.

Brenner, N. (2009). 'What is critical urban theory?' *City*, 13(2–3), 198–207. https://doi.org/10.1080/13604810902996466

Gieryn, T.F. (2006). City as Truth-Spot. *Social Studies of Science*, 36(1), 5–38.

Hunter, A. (1980). Why Chicago? The Rise of the Chicago School of Urban Social Science. *The American Behavioral Scientist (Beverly Hills)*, 24(2), 215–227.

Lefebvre, H. (1991). *The Production of Space*. Oxford UK / Cambridge USA: Blackwell Publishing.

Lopes de Souza, M. (2012). Marxists, libertarians and the city. *City*, 16(3), 315–331.

Lutters, W. and Ackerman, M. (1996). An Introduction to the Chicago School of Sociology. *Interval Research Proprietary*.

Mallarmé, S. (1898). Le Livre. In Schérer, Jacques, *Le Livre de Mallarmé*. Paris: Gallimard, 1957.

Niculae, Lorin, Jorge Mejía Hernández, Klaske Havik, Mark Proosten (2021). Narrative Methods for Writing Urban Places. *Writingplace Journal* issue #5. Rotterdam: nai010publishers https://journals.open.tudelft.nl/writingplace/issue/view/878

Roy, A. (2016). Who's Afraid of Postcolonial Theory?. *International Journal of Urban and Regional Research*, 40(1), 200–209.

Tuana, N. (2017). Feminist Epistemology. In *The Routledge Handbook of Epistemic Injustice* (125–138). London: Routledge.

Introduction

Instructions on How to Roam into this Repository – or not.

This Repository can work as a book of recipes, providing alternative strategies for writing urban places, with steps you could try out, while always allowing for many possible combinations. As this is not a regular book (nor a regular building), you don't need to read it linearly, from cover to cover, or to go all over every alley from the entrance to the exit, rather:

Pre-assignment

1
Draw up your own itinerary choosing the methods and procedures that are related to the subjects you are interested in, to the media you are familiar with, to the scopes you want to achieve, to the forms of implementation you want to try.

2
Venture yourself through unknown alleys… and create as many itineraries as you want or need, combining the familiar with the unfamiliar.

3
Use the blank spaces (empty shelves) to write or draw your own notes and comments about the methods and procedures you are interested in, or to make the assignments proposed by our contributors; feel free to paste photos, or maps, or journal clippings, or whatever comes to your mind.

4
Do you have something to add to one of the methods or a suggestion to make on references or further readings in order to deepen the latter? Do not hesitate to complete the online version of the Repository (this is an open and interactive book, a building in permanent construction. You have an active role in the continuity of its realisation).

5
Did you find a method that is somehow related to the project you are working on? Why don't you make some copies of the assignment proposed by the author of this particular method and develop it with your colleagues or with your students, in your agency, laboratory or class?

6
Do you think several methods could be complementary? Try to combine them in order to generate a hybrid one. That invitation works also for the assignments: you can graft and assemble parts of different assignments and create a hyper-assignment.

pre-assignment

7
Do you think somebody across the world (a colleague, a friend, a relative) could be interested in one of the assignments you found in the book? Or in an implementation you just made of one of them? Take a post-card, fill it with your proposition, go to the nearest post office, buy a stamp, and send it to that person.

8
Do not worry if this Repository's wear starts to be noticeable: if some important lines are underlined with ink, borders are bent, some sheets are missing, or the covers are ripped. It is meant to be used and reused, as paths that can be walked, over and over again, in different directions, finding new views on the way.

method

Appraising

Transactions between architectures

Jorge Mejía Hernández
Faculty of Architecture and the Built Environment,
Delft University of Technology

The method of architectural transaction analysis is inspired by works of art that approach reality as a series of interrelations, such as the Chinese *I Ching*, Hesse's *Glass Bead Game*, or Mark Lombardi's drawings. At a methodological level, it evolves from architectural approaches to Imre Lakatos' sophisticated explanation of the different exchanges that explain scientific discovery according to Popper. From this perspective, knowledge results from formulating hypotheses and evaluating our experience through them in conflict and collaboration with others, rather than in isolation. Thus, the use of the word, 'transaction,' to name this method recognises: (a) the economic rationality of exchange, (b) relevant psychological aspects of human interaction, and (c) the importance of recording said exchanges and interactions. In line with this interpretation, rather than focusing on the nature and performance of a single building, the method examines differences and similarities between two or more of them. It is not necessary that these are in any way similar or coeval. In fact, a transaction analysis of quite-different buildings is usually rewarding. It is crucial however, that it is possible to compare multiple representations of each of the transacting buildings in order to acknowledge their poly-technical nature and performance.

A first stage of analysis abstracts the same distinct aspect in each transacting building, documents it as completely as possible, and links it to documented or reasonably inferred decisions which were (possibly) made by their creators within a discrete field of architectural exploration, evaluation, and discovery – also referred to as a positive heuristic. Transaction analysis presumes that every building results from poly-technical decisions made in four distinct heuristics, namely: (a) form and configuration, (b) use, purpose, and performance, (c) technique, materiality and construction, and (c) communication, and meaning.

Given its basis in falsification, this method is neither aimed towards conclusive truths nor reliant on incontrovertible assumptions. Instead, it can be used to reconstruct a number of plausible decision-making

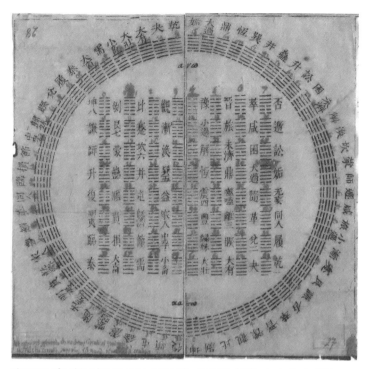

Diagram of I Ching hexagrams owned by Gottfried Wilhelm Leibniz, 1701. (Source: Wikimedia Commons)

processes and to analyse salient aspects of them systematically. Singled-out decisions made by different architects within each positive heuristic can be compared and contrasted as transactions between different buildings, both rigorously and creatively. By abstracting different design decisions, localising their outcomes within clearly demarcated heuristics, and recognising them as equivalent, the method makes apparently unrelated architectures comparable, regardless of their time or place. Evidence-based accounts of two or more decision-making processes developed with this method constitute valuable operative knowledge for the study and practice of buildings and cities.

As an abstractive method, architectural transaction analysis is not only useful to explain the growth and development of knowledge in the built environment; it is also instrumental to overcome limitations in our understanding of architecture and the city that result from the classification of buildings in fixed categories or hierarchies, and their ascription to any particular identity or culture.

Appraising

References

Anderson, S. (1984). Architectural Design as a System of Research Programs. *Design Studies*, 5(3), 146-150.

Hesse, H. (1973). *The Glass Bead Game*. Penguin Books.

I Ching. (2003) trans. Richard Wilhelm. London: Penguin Books.

Lakatos, I. (1978) *The Methodology of Scientific Research Programmes*. Cambridge University Press.

Landau, R. (1982). Methodology of Research Programs. In B. Evans, J.A. Powell, & R. Talbot (Eds.), *Changing Design*, London: John Wiley and Sons, 303-309.

Lombardi, M. Artist's page in the MoMA collection, https://www.moma.org/artists/22980, accessed May 4, 2022.

Martí Arís, C. (2021). *Variations of Identity: Type in Architecture*. Editions Cosa Mentale.

Mejía Hernández, J. (2018). *Transactions; or Architecture as a System of Research Programs*, PhD dissertation. TU Delft.

Motta, G. and Pizzigoni, A. (2008). *La Máquina de Proyecto*. Bogotá Universidad Nacional de Colombia.

Popper, K. (2022). *The Logic of Scientific Discovery*. London: Routledge.

Assignment

1
Define a starting hypothesis regarding a particular aspect of the built environment you want to observe. For example: the implantation and shape of a building can produce a radically disorienting effect in human perception.

2
Select two or more buildings that appear to contain valuable knowledge pertaining to that aspect. For example: It appears that some Pre-Columbine architectures from Mesoamerica; a library by Rogelio Salmona, and a museum by SANAA, share this disorienting property.

3
Analyse each building individually by abstracting, via different representations, specific qualities which can be examined and evaluated on their own. For example: It is clear that the height of some Mesoamerican platforms is exactly that of the surrounding treetops. Salmona also defines the height of his courtyards at the exact height required to block the view of all surrounding buildings; and SANAA make a slight, almost imperceptible curve in the layout of their main gallery that produces abnormal reflections of light in walls and windows. These characteristics can be observed in plan and cross-section drawings of these buildings.

4

Organise analytical findings in terms of the observed reality's formal, functional, constructive and communicative performance. For example: The above decisions are all related to the size and shape of these buildings, and therefore fit within the formal heuristic of architecture. Their effects are perceptual, showing how decisions made in the formal heuristic have consequences in the buildings' use, purpose, or performance.

5

Compare and contrast results among observed realities, per heuristic category. For example: While platforms and courtyards block some visible aspects of reality in order to reveal them suddenly once the user's position changes, SANAA introduces an additional distortion in perception by using reflective materials like stainless steel and glass.

6

Based on the results of each transaction, revise initial or formulate new hypotheses, or apply results to develop a new built environment. For example: From the transaction analysis of these three architectures we can conclude that the formal strategies used by Mayan architects and Rogelio Salmona to produce a disorienting effect can be developed further by the use of subtle curves and reflective materials, as suggested by SANAA.

The use of transactional analysis can be considered successful if it reveals unknown, unexpected, unforeseen, or unrealised aspects of reality; or if it offers improved forms of understanding to the initial hypothesis and/or the observed built environments.

Assembling Pasts

Retrospective narration in place analysis

Kinga Kimic
Department of Landscape Architecture,
Warsaw University of Life Sciences

Narration is the oral or written action that undertakes the telling of an event or a series of events; it refers to the reconstruction (chronological or not) of real or fictitious events through the discursive device. Of particular significance within the narrative possibilities, is 'Retrospective narration'. Retrospective narration occurs when the event being told is not happening at the time the narrator is telling it, and it may be carried out by a character present within the story or by a third-person omniscient narrator.

The diverse of forms of retrospective narration include short, thematic stories (e.g. notes, comments, poems, etc.), long descriptions (records from diaries, records from travels and excursions, books, etc.), and even press articles about events, places, and specific characters.

Retrospective narration is one of the most representative metods to document the past. It is a form of communication rooted in time and space, and a source of information as well as a cognitive and educational tool implemented in many interdisciplinary areas, including those related to writing places. It may focus on physical features and elements making up the place, but, through a narrator's impressions, feelings and opinions, it may describe the '*genius loci*' (its exceptional identity and its spiritual character) of a place as well.

However, these descriptions of the past have not only a historical value as a form of documentation or commemoration; this specific form of communication can be easily developed into a wider perspective of time – showing the past in relation to the present and also anticipating the future. The characteristics of a place as discovered and gathered through retrospective narration become a form of evidence of its history. Such reports can also be consciously compared and assessed from today's point of view, increasing the scope of relations between time and narrative. The comparison of collected information with other sources (cartographies, photographs, and descriptions) related to different time periods may increase the knowledge about the place and, integrating the unchanging and the changeable elements, it could support the evaluation processes allowing to better plan its development, restoration, reconstruction, and conservation (or even its destruction).

Retrospective narration may support historical analyses and comparisons with other sources of the place at the present (using photographic documentation and other descriptions).

For example, in a study of the Planty Krakowskie Park in Kraków, Poland, we identified the most valuable elements – physical and immaterial – in a paper published in 1912 by Gustaw Pol. From the historical source, we found relevant information about the role of 'Planty' park in the city and its main natural elements, about the park arrangement including its linear form and about its main equipment and buildings, we learned about dendrological aspects of the park, about flower beds as characterising elements, and about the monuments in the park. The retrospective narration of this source, assembling aspects of the park's past, revealed the diversity of meanings within the park, which led to its subsequent successful restoration.

References

Pol, G. (1912). *Spacer letni po plantach krakowskich* [A summer walk along Planty Krakowskie park – in Polish]. *Ogrodnictwo*, 11, 1912, 327-330.

Further Reading

Altman, R. (2008). *A Theory of Narrative*. New York: Columbia University Press.

Cierka, A. & Dryll, E. (ed). (2004). *Narracja. Koncepcje i badania psychologiczne* [Narration. Concepts and psychological research]. Warszawa: Wydawnictwo Instytutu Psychologii PAN.

Dobson, M. & Ziemann, B. (2020). *Reading Primary Sources: The Interpretation of Texts from Nineteenth and Twentieth Century History*. London: Routledge.

Genette, G. (1980). *Narrative Discourse: An Essay in Method*. New York: Cornell University Press.

Malecki, B. (1903). *Plantacye krakowskie* [Planty Krakowskie park]. *Ogrodnictwo*, 3, 1903, 67-71.

Ricoeur, P. (1990). *Time and Narrative*. Translated by Kathleen McLaughlin and David Pellauer. Chicago and London: University of Chicago Press.

Stenzel, F.K. (1986). *A Theory of Narrative*. Translated by Charlotte Goedsche. Cambridge, New York: Cambridge University Press.

Assembling Pasts

Assignment

1
Select a place or an area with a long history (a square, a park, a district or a part of it etc.) in the city where you live or you are visiting.

2
Search for a description of this place related to its history, using sources such as diaries, poems, records from travels or excursions, etc. Use online sources or visit the local library.

3
Study the text in detail: select the most important spatial elements of the place, learn about their history, characteristics, and the narrator's individual impressions, feelings and opinions.

4
Before visiting the place, plan a walk and mark the selected objects on a map (printed or digital).

5
Go for a visit alone or with your friends and start the exploration of the place. Find the objects previously selected and compare them with the historical description. In the case of an object that no longer exists or have been destroyed, try to find their former location and/or their remnants, and identify what has changed about them.

6
Write down your own description, taking into account the current situation of the place. Use the same narration form of the writing you chose (diary, story, poem, etc.).

7
Now, focus on your own feelings and add them to your description. Do the historical elements evoke feelings in you like those of the narrator of the text you chose?

8
Assemble the description you chose and studied, and the one you wrote in order to grasp the evolution of the '*genius loci*' of the place over time.

Atlasing Urban Experience

Site visits through unfolding place

Caendia Wijnbelt
Faculty of Architecture and Landscape Sciences, Leibniz University, Hannover

In architectural practices, even in research-driven environments, site visits are often one-off events; sites and projects are mostly visited on single occasions. In contrast, 'Atlasing' is a way of keeping trace of a broad number of site realities encountered; a way of tracing over time which combines repeated fieldwork with reflexive practices that can be characteristic of research. *Atlases of urban experience* are adaptive and can be used in a variety of scenarios as tools for bettering our understanding of places in the city.

This method focuses on the process of making and reading map-like handmade compositions: folding and unfolding the resulting pieces is a way of shifting between a focus on specific fragments and a broader overview, allowing a bird's-eye view. This approach can accompany anyone interested in fieldwork focusing on built and lived environments, opening to narrative as well as reflexive research strategies that promote plural readings and interpretations – a modality of threading together urban stories with more flexibility, openness, and imagination.

As a large-format folding logbook, the result of such Atlasing resembles the shape of most old travel fold-out maps: cartographic tools that the user tends to handle not-so-carefully in the field – sometimes scrutinising a tiny section of the folded paper, sometimes spreading it out, arms wide open to get a glimpse of a whole journey. The folding and unfolding operation is key to making and reading these atlases. Such activities set in varying relation what is, at first sight, deemed relevant (through fieldnotes) with what might have otherwise gone unnoticed (through more intuitive composite drawings), producing new dynamics.

The multimedium map combines fieldnotes (therefore chronological) on the upper sections, and more intuitive and fluid interpretations that are neither site – nor time-bound below – through photographic series about light, letters to an imaginary user, or painted explorations of the city's emotional topographies to mention only a few possibilities.

Places have fleeting and moving features and so do not fit within a strict methodological framing, but rather encourage case-by-case specifications. One challenge, therefore, is to refine the methodological steps for each new iteration of such a prototype. A fourteen-day observation of a small windowsill habitat might result in a very different atlas than that of a park or building visited across four different seasons. Modes of writing, drawing, or photographing – as well as focuses – are thereby iterative yet case-specific components of the *atlases*.

Acknowledgement
This is a method developed in the ongoing PhD project: 'Sketching Mindscapes. Place and reflexivity in architectural design', Caendia Wijnbelt (LUH).

Assignment

1
Choose a street to visit as many times as you have columns in your blank fold-out map over the next few weeks.

2
On each trip, chronologically fill one section in the upper part of the map with fieldnotes, sketches, photographs, time stamps etc. that you've noticed and documented on site.

3
Independently of this top half, fill the bottom half with drawn, written or other forms of reflections which come to mind while thinking about the site you chose.

4
These reflective drawings can be taken up and continued at any moment on site, or after the fact, folding and unfolding the lower half of the accordion according to how the composition takes shape.

5
Once the atlasing process is paused, take some time to manipulate it. Read it sequentially, by unfolding the accordion day by day, comparing the upper fieldnotes to the fragment of the drawn composition beneath it. Read the upper part of the atlas as a whole: the chronological fieldnotes as narration of the site. Next, read the lower part in its entirety, as a composed, multimedia reflection of the site. Unfold the entire atlas. How has your perception evolved over the visits? How do these readings afford different impressions of the experience? Try to name different features of the street that can be perceived through each kind of reading.

6
Consider the resulting fold-out-map as an open, evolving sheet of paper. Although you may have decided it is completed, each feature could of course be further explored and extrapolated. What could you add a year later? How could this period of atlasing a fragment of the city inform and connect with other experiences, and other streets?

assignment

Bordering

Observational walks along edges

Mattias Malk
Estonian Academy of Arts, Tallinn

Doreen Massey has thought considerably about how to make sense of place. She makes clear that in an era of mobility and circulation, a sense of place must also reflect these experiences (Massey, 1993). So instead of clear boundaries which isolate and specify them, places are progressive and increasingly defined by their interactions with other places. In her work she references her own neighbourhood of Kilburn in London (Massey, 1991) and how the shift towards a progressive sense of place has enabled her to study this otherwise rather ordinary place from a planetary perspective. The method of 'bordering' does not do away with the concept of boundaries altogether. Instead, it applies the lens of exchange and dynamics to exploring, defining and critiquing the idea of a place as something authentic or rooted in a singular history.

One way to apply this method could be to take an official map of the place you are studying and to walk along its outline. For a housing project or neighbourhood, this could take minutes or hours. Applied to whole metropolitan areas, this could become a durational walk in the spirit of the Stalker Group, where researchers stay embedded in the field for days (see Careri, 2001; Lang, 2006). Another way could be to investigate natural borders such as coastlines, rivers or cliffs and trace those across your field. Regardless of the chosen border, your attention should be directed towards the potentialities and dynamics this border creates, rather than the act of delineation. What does the border make (im)possible? Who is in, who is out and when? It is important to have the tools on hand to record these observations on the go, so that they can be meaningfully reproduced and studied.

The added benefit of this methodology is its reproducibility. When applied in a variety of contexts the insights have great comparative potential. Depending on the accompanying method of recording and reproduction, the method could be useful for researching urban identities, segregation, housing inequality, peripheries, mobility, or migra-

Walks with students on the borders of Tallinn. Photo: Mattias Malk.

tion, among other topics. The specific outcome of this methodology relies on the site and chosen recording technique. A more general outcome could be situated knowledge of how a place is defined.

References
Careri, F. (2001). Transborderline. *Architectural Design* 71(3), 87-91.

Lang, P. (2006). Stalker on Location. In Franck, Karen A. & Stevens, Quentin (Eds.) *Loose Space: Possibility and Diversity in Urban Life*, Routledge, 193-209.

Massey, D. (1991). A Global Sense of Place. *Marxism Today* (38), 24-29.

Massey, D. (1993). Power-geometry and a progressive sense of place. In *Mapping the Futures*, Routledge, 75-85.

Examples
Alÿs, Francis (2004) The Green Line. Jerusalem, Israel.

Stalker / Osservatorio Nomade.

Assignment

1
Define your area of study and choose a border to investigate. This could be an administrative border, it could be defined with participative mapping methods, it could be subliminal, or it could be an aspect of the natural environment. Whatever the criteria, a general definition (even if flawed at its inception) of a place is a necessary precondition and yardstick for this method. A neighbourhood or a city centre would be a convenient example.

2
Decide on a route and a method to use for note taking and/or field recording. The route could be circular or linear. The recording method could be a notepad, a Dictaphone, a stills camera, a video camera or all of them rolled into a smartphone. In a group, the task of recording can be shared.

3
Before beginning the walk, it is a good idea to write down your expectations. What do you think you will find? What is the official narrative or prejudice about your field?

4
Allow yourself adequate time for the journey and for experiencing any specific places along the act of bordering. Decide if overnight stays are necessary and if these are a part of the fieldwork.

5
Try to pay particular attention to the kinds of exchange and interactions which constitute the border. Note down anything meaningful along the way, even if it does not immediately relate to your research interests.

6
Pay particular attention to your personal reflections and record these unfiltered and as much as possible.

7
If you find your attention slipping, try to understand why. Are you simply fatigued or has the place itself impressed this on you?

8
At the end of the walk, gather your findings and organise them. Reflect on the information, edit and systematise for representation. How did the border-field differ from your initial expectations?

assignment

Building Consensus on Place Representation

method

Lorin Niculae, Irina Scobiola, Bogdan Guiu and Dragoș Gherghescu
Ion Mincu, University of Architecture and Urbanism, Bucharest

The social representation of place presents a system of values, notions, and practices, relative to a place, that organise the perception of the place and formulate social answers. It is also a process of converting the place into symbolic categories (of values and beliefs) with cognitive status, which, by integrating the self into social interaction, allow understanding (Moscovici, 2019). Such representation requires an evaluation apparatus, a situation in the world of values, a transcription of place by means of each individual philosophy of life as validated by the community. Finally, social representation has a meaning which is obtained by the inherent subjectivation of the group itself.

This participatory method of identifying the social representation of place has four major functions:
1 To read and understand a place.
2 To define the identity of place and understand the specificity of the groups that define a certain place.
3 To orient and inform behaviour and practices.
4 To justify, a posteriori, the decisions taken.

To study a social representation of a place together with community members means to study its structure; the way the elements that form the representation interact and position themselves among the others (Moliner, 1993). The elements remembered and recognised by the majority of the investigating community members stand as 'core' elements, while others, less important, are marginal. The research will determine the importance of each element and identify the rank of the core elements. The more an element is central (present in many descriptions of the group members), the more characteristic it is for the place. Hence, changing several particular core elements of a representation can trigger the change of the representation itself. The attributes of the core elements are: symbolic value, associative power, relevance, association and connectivity (Moliner, 1993).

The method needs a group for executing the analysis, which should be practiced in the early analysis stage of site investigation. The larger the group, the more consistent the findings will be. Each

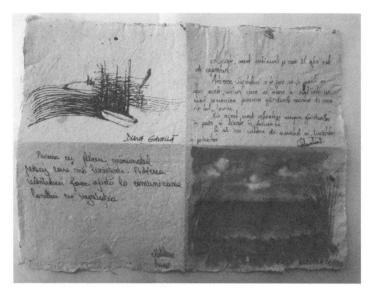

Associative folding using the technique of the ambiguous scenario (Moliner, 1993) of cross-remembering. Photo: Lorin Niculae

member of the group writes at least 5 characteristics that define a recently visited place, in order of their importance. Then, these characteristics (elements of the representation) are organised in a table which will show their rank (order) and position (how many times has it been mentioned by the participants).
For example, as experimented with the students of IMUAU, Bucharest, the found emotions and important visual elements of the place (existing, remembered and/or imagined) can be transcribed on an affective map of the place.

The purpose of the method is to create an assembly of core elements that create the meaning of the place, gathered by consensus of the participating community members. Changing those specific elements means to change the representation and, consequently, the meaning of the place. The method is particularly useful when architects and urbanists need to understand which parts of the place need to change and which need to be preserved, in order to improve the quality of the place and preserve its identity and value. As a result, in the next step of the proces an urban intervention will focus on these particular elements and use them as important concepts that inform the design.

References

Abric, J.-C. (1994). Methodologie de recueil des representations sociales, in J.-C. Abric (ed.). *Pratiques sociales et representations*, Paris: PUF.

Jodelet, D. (ed.). (2003). *Les Representations Sociales. Collection: "Sociologie d'aujourd'hui"*. Paris: Presses Universitaires de France.

Moliner, P. (1993). ISA: L'induction par Scenario Ambiguu, Une methode pour l'etude des representations sociales, *Revue Internationale de Psychologie Sociale*, no. 2, 7-21.

Moscovici, S. (2019). *Psychologie des représentations sociales*, Paris: Editions des Archives contemporaines.

Further Readings

Abric, J.-C. (1989). L'étude experimentale des representations sociales, in D. Jodelet (ed.). *Les Representations Sociales*. Collection : "Sociologie d'aujourd'hui". Paris : Les Presses universitaires de France.

Batel, S., Castro P. (2018). Reopening the dialogue between the theory of social representations and discursive psychology for examining the construction and transformation of meaning in discourse and communication. *British Journal of Social Psychology* 57: 732–53, https://bpspsychub.onlinelibrary.wiley.com/doi/epdf/10.1111/bjso.12259

Rubira-García, R., Puebla-Martínez, B., Gelado-Marcos, R. (2018). Social Representations in Studying Information, Knowledge, and Mediations: A Critical Review, *Soc. Sci.* 2018, 7(12), 256;https://www.mdpi.com/2076-0760/7/12/256

Assignment

1
Form an analysis group of 5-15 community members.

2
Do a transect walk of the place.

3
Collect data: visual and narrative recordings. Describe the place.

4
Pay attention to emotions and important visual elements of the place (existing, remembered and/or imagined) and transcribe them on an affective map of the place.

5
Identify the important emotions and memories from step 4 and organise the data in a table, in order to determine the rank of the elements and their position within the 'core' elements of the representation.

6
Verify the core elements on the affective map and update the map.

7
Create pairings of words and images (Abric, 1994). See Figure.

8
Use the core elements to inform the urban or architectural design through the filter of individual and collective axiology.

Characterising Details

Classification of unique characteristics in historic sites

Juan A. García-Esparza
Universitat Jaume I, Castelló

Identity, culture, authenticity, and integrity define the character of a place and are all inherent values in heritage and landscape perception. Many current placemaking approaches to heritage contexts are called to be participatory and inclusive. The method presented here attempts to qualitatively study historic built environments during the early stages of evaluation to better understand their values. Although the character assessment of architectural and social values in historic urban cores may come from global forms of appraisal, the ultimate objective is to make locals the protagonists of conservation, stewards of intangible values, and legitimate decision-makers. Therefore, this method focuses on strengthening the unique characteristics of historic sites on a local level, avoiding broad assumptions and focusing on the minor variances that occur within a specific area.

This approach involves residents in the analysis of cultural heritage components and practices to establish the overall characteristics of local architecture and the everyday life of historic districts. This shared view of sites rests on the historical, architectural, and ethnographic qualities and stimulates the current forms of engagement with the site. Neighbours may express questions and concerns about conservation and development during workshops, which may then be linked to tourism, transportation, and amenities, all of which influence their habitat. Answers may denote current anxieties and peculiarities associated with space habitation.

Together with local residents, this method employs street-view analysis and aims to catalogue forms of expression, particularly the existence of specific elements in façades, openings, carpentry, balconies, and fences. The components to be categorised and registered need a preliminary phase of visual identification through site inspections. These inspections can be carried out collectively, with neighbours, or individually by researchers.

A collection of architectural values in the form of arts and crafts. Historical, Cultural, and Tangible Values. Study's first phase (2020). Author's source.

The manual classification and registration is carried out on-site utilising printed cadastral maps. Fieldwork allows researchers to categorise and quantify the components of interest in different areas and districts and visually correlate them. At this stage, further contact with local institutions may serve to contrast information regarding protection plans and significance or protection levels.

Photo-elicitation workshops provide images of locations representative of the values of the area to highlight their importance and the ties people had with those places. Photo-elicitation is not a replacement for complementary analysis such as interviews; instead, it is an add-on activity that provides legitimacy and depth. In addition, the capacity of informants to articulate their practical knowledge through the attribution and connection of meanings is stimulated by photo-elicitation. In these activities, informants provide information about their views of certain events and the values they assign to them.

Characterising Details

Acknowledgement
This method has been developed as part of a larger project: *Writing historic centres. Dynamics of contemporary place-making in Spanish World Heritage Cities.* DoCplaceS.

References
García-Esparza, J.A. (2019). Beyond the intangible-tangible binary in cultural heritage. An analysis from rural areas in Valencia Region, Spain. *International Journal of Intangible Heritage*, 14 (1), 123-137.

García-Esparza, J.A., Altaba, P. (2020). A GIS-based Methodology for the Appraisal of Historical, Architectural and Social Values in Historic Urban Cores. *Frontiers of Architectural Research* 9 (4), 900-913.

García-Esparza, J.A. (2022). Urban Scene Protection and Unconventional Practices - Contemporary Landscapes in World Heritage Cities of Spain. *Land* 11 (3), 324. second.wiki/wiki/liste_der_strac39fen_und_plc3a4tze_von_kc3b6nigsberg_1905. Last accessed: 21/01/2022

Assignment

1
Form a group of researchers and local residents of the historic site in question. Define the site to be inspected.

2
Street-view analysis/site inspection: walk in the streets and take photos and sketches of architectural details, specific elements in façades, openings, carpentry, balconies, and fences.

3
Explain, discuss, and manually classify and register your findings on-site through printed cadastral maps.

Charting People, Activities, and Places

Present Map workshop in public spaces

Kestutis Zaleckis, Jurga Vitkuviene, Laura Jankauskaite-Jureviciene, Indre Grazuleviciute-Vileniske, Kaunas University of Technology.

Vilma Karvelyte-Balbieriene, Kaunas University of Technology / Kaunas City Municipality.

The Present Map methodology is designed for three purposes: to collect material about people's experiences in public spaces of the locality; to empower the community by providing the working tools and platform for expression; to connect the community with the place through direct experience and the typological knowledge about the public spaces and their usage.

The methodology integrates the tools and philosophies from psychogeography, sociotope methodology, and design thinking approach. The mental mapping technique (Gieseking, 2013) is integrated within psychogeography; the typology of activities and the concept of the public space as a "biotope" is taken from sociotope methodology (Laszkiewicz et al., 2020); the design thinking approach (International Design Foundation, 2019) provided the idea of using hands-on techniques and involving drawing, colouring, cutting, and gluing activities.

The Present Map methodology is implemented in the form of mapping workshops and can be organised as follows. First, the workshop coordinator provides general information about the intended activities and presents themes related to public space, such as typologies, different activities, and potential users. Then, groups of 4-6 participants are formed that collectively draw the locality from memory on an A1 (or larger) sheet of paper. Subsequently, working groups walk and explore the locality to identify public spaces and trace people, activities and/or signs of activities. Afterwards, groups locate the places in a geographical map of the locality, identifying and marking found objects and places from their collective drawings made during the fieldwork, adding comments about features of these places and objects. In the geographical map, groups identify the activities they spotted during the fieldworks as well as distinguished places and different users. Here, participants are informed about different kinds of activities and users. Activities can be subdivided as follows: a) active: swimming, ball games, and sports in general; b) passive: relaxation in nature, flower observation, sitting; c) events: organised happenings and celebrations; d) other: activities spotted by the participants. Different users can be identified as: adults, seniors, youngsters, adolescents, school age children, preschool children, parents or other care takers with children, special needs people, tourists, uniformed officials. Activities are marked with sticky notes and users with pictogram stickers.

Following this mapping session, all groups share and compare information and experiences with other groups. Individually, participants fill the online interactive map (Genius Loci, 2022) entering selected experiences from the physical map onto the interactive map using a computer or mobile device. The workshop concludes with a general discussion. To kick-off the discussion, the moderator may ask: 'What kind of places did your group identify? Who visited them and what were they doing? Which places were exceptional and why? Which kind of activities were happening and where?' The moderator can also ask if participants note "blank spots" of the locality and why they think these spots are blank. To wrap up the discussion, moderators may ask which place participants remember the most and why they believe this place is important.

The tangible outcomes of the workshop are: collective drawings of the locality by the workshop participants, information about the identified places and their users, as well as activities or signs of activities within these localities. Furthermore, the participants produce a geographical map of the locality with identified public spaces and the users and activities of these spaces, alongside entering information into the online interactive present map.

References

Genius Loci. https://sanciubendruomene.lt/en/ (11 01 2022)

Gieseking, J. J. (2013). Where We Go from Here: The Mental Sketch Mapping Method and Its Analytic Components. *Qualitative Inquiry*, 19(9), 712–724.

International Design Foundation. 5 Stages in the Design Thinking Process (2019). https://www.interaction-design.org/literature/article/5-stages-in-the-design-thinking-process

Laszkiewicz, E., Czembrowski, P., Kronenberg J. (2020). Creating a Map of the Social Functions of Urban Green Spaces in a City with Poor Availability of Spatial Data: A Sociotope for Lodz. *Land* 9(6), 183; doi:10.3390/land9060183

Assignment

The material, required for the workshop includes flip-chart paper, sticky notes, in advance prepared pictogram stickers, pens, pencils and markers, glue and scissors, printed geographical maps of the locality, hand-out material for the fieldwork and the interactive online map for data collection (Genius Loci, 2022). Human resources necessary for the workshops are the workshop coordinator and moderators. One moderator can work with 4-5 groups of participants. The workshop is implemented in several steps, which can be classified into: 1) general information for all participants and other introductory activities including the formation of working groups, 2) working in groups, 3) sharing of information, presentations, generalizations, and discussions, 4) individual work. The exemplary assignment for the group work is presented below:

Group work - collective drawing of locality from memory

1
Makegroups of 4 to 6 participants.

2
The moderator must present the wide array of places that fall under the typology of public spaces: from the parks and streets to publicly accessible courtyards, cemeteries, and riversides.

3
Participants are handed an A1 (or larger) sheet of paper and, in groups, will draw the map of the locality from memory.

4
To initiate the drawing process, the moderator can ask the following questions: 'Which public spaces and places do you know in the locality? What are the places you visit the most often? What are the places you hear about the most often?' etc.

5
The drawing may involve street networks, buildings, public spaces, green structures, water bodies. The participants should add comments to each drawn object - name or title, related recent memories, and/or the mood of the place.

6
During the drawing process, the moderator may ask the following questions: 'What is this place? What is characteristic to this place? Who visits this place? What are people doing in this place?'.

7
As a whole group, participants reflect and discuss what they learned from and about the locality and its public spaces by drawing together.

assignment

Co-creating

Workshop
Arquitecturas Colectivas

method

Yazmín M. Crespo Claudio, Omayra Rivera Crespo and Irmaris Santiago Rodríguez, Taller Creando Sin Encargo

"The white fathers told us, I think therefore I am; and the black mothers in each of us -the poet- whispers in our dreams, I feel therefore I can be free." (Lorde 1984, p.3 8)

Making theories and proposing a practice from a feminist perspective of architectural design and urbanism implies a decolonial position as well. Knowledge must be situated in community initiatives and intersectional experiences, in inclusive and multidisciplinary pedagogy, and in the constant negotiation of the public space despite precariousness resulting from a neoliberal approach. Workshop, *Arquitecturas Colectivas*, is an inclusive methodology created by the all-women design collective *taller Creando Sin Encargos* [Yazmín M. Crespo Claudio, Dra. Omayra Rivera Crespo, and Irmaris Santiago Rodríguez], that encourages the exchange of knowledge at the horizontal level and looks at how design and architecture can have agency in the ideation and construction of spaces together with students, volunteers, and the community. The approach, based on participatory action research, focuses on two placemaking methods: creative activism, and mechanics of building. Creative activism facilitates the engagement of active citizens by designing a hands-on exercise to address the project. Mechanics of building studies matter within the context of the community by including local initiatives, communication strategies, and local building methods.

The workshop begins with a toolkit; addressing the agency of space that exhibits a two-part tactic. The framework and method of engagements *in situ*. The framework must always be made to observe the context, primarily spatial and human relations. It is important to seek other organisations and groups that are already working with the community, as well as to participate in community meetings, build relationships with community leaders, and learn about their concerns and goals. The result will be an activity that address the community's interest and the project's extent. The process is documented with photography, drawings, notes, and video.

Workshop Arquitecturas Colectivas III, 2021.
Photo: Taller Creando Sin Encargos

From framing to co-creating, the method is co-designed and built-in situ. The project is designed on site collectively with residents, students, and volunteers. Drawings are made/remade after slow observations of the context and responding to everyone's input. Likewise, modifications are accepted during construction so that the design is organic and inclusive. Ask the locals! Reach out to community members for material resources, labour, food services, among others. After construction, there is a round table or conversation to reflect on the objectives and concerns, construction process, possible programming, and responsibilities towards the space.

The Workshop is thought of more as an archipelago, where participatory solidarity, collective architectures, and popular tactics are part of the desired daily life. Building locally is critical to making real change. The project incorporates power into place, meaning that *in situ* is a place where effect situates change through the empowerment of others.

References
Lorde. A. (1984). *Sister outsider: essays and speeches*. Canada: Crossing Press.

Crespo, Y., Rivera, O., & Santiago, I. (2021b). Haciendo teorías: TOOLkit desde perspectivas feministas Caribeñas. *XXXV Jornadas de Investigación de la Facultad de Arquitectura, Diseño y Urbanismo en Buenos Aires Argentina*, FADU UBA, Argentina. October 4-7, Actas SI + Palabras Clave, 2433-2448

Co-creating

Further readings

Crespo, Y., Rivera, O., & Santiago, I. (2021a). Performing Architectures: 'haciendo teorías' [making room] for situated narratives of design. *27th World Congress of Architects: UIA Rio 2021 & ACSA International Conference. Rio de Janeiro, Brazil.* July 18-22. Paper Proceedings Vol 1. https://www.acsa-arch.org/chapter/performing-architectures-haciendo-teor...

Crespo, Y., Rivera, O., & Santiago, I. (2020). Urbanismo de Resistencia en Puerta de Tierra: II Workshop Arquitecturas Colectivas. *Bitácora Urbano Territorial.* Universidad Nacional de Colombia Sede Bogotá Facultad de Artes Volumen 30 No. 1, 51-60.

Crespo, Y., & Rivera, O. (2026). WORKSHOP Collectives Architectures. *ACSA International Conference, Santiago, Chile.* June 26 - July 1. Cross Americas: Probing Disglobal Networks Proceedings.

Assignment

1
Observe the framework of reference: conduct 10-to-15-minute self-tours/detours and guided walks through the city/neighbourhood with all participants and community members, especially the children. In this way, it is possible to see the neighbourhood from the point of view of its residents. As you walk, ask the participants about stories of places, and actions. Help the children identify people, objects, events, and verbs.

2
Start a process of exchanging knowledge and experiences through dialogue. To prompt this exchange, carry out a storytelling session.

3
Ask the residents (often the children are the primary users of public spaces) to write and/or draw how they remember inhabiting the spaces, and how they would like to inhabit them. Here, memories and imagination come together in a single story.

4
Based on the storytelling session, the drawings, and the texts, collectively translate memories and desires so that they become inhabitable spaces. Verbs that become actions and adjectives that become spatial qualities can be extracted from these stories.

5
With this, plans and elevations are drawn for the residents to confirm they exhibit the spaces they visualise.

6
Then, develop the drawings together to reflect the place they want to inhabit.

7
What did you learn about the spaces/places by listening to the people's stories?

Collaging Community Narratives

Jeremy Allan Hawkins
École Nationale Supérieure d'Architecture de Strasbourg

The principles of collage are seemingly simple: by assembling previously unrelated figures together in a field, a new composition is formed. As a creative practice, it offers a unique approach to producing encounters and bringing dissimilar materials, ideas, and positions into conversation. In this sense, the collage artist is always working in a pluri-vocal or multitimbral form. What Mikhail Bakhtin considered to be a polyphonic and/or dialogic relationship to language in Dostoevsky's novels through the representation of multiple voices is, in collage, rather a principle of composition itself, with the different "voices" literally assembled in the new work.

Much like the city, the disparate constitutive elements of a collage are brought into juxtaposition and dialogue without negating or effacing them. Significant aspects or even the integral wholes of the source material can be maintained in collage, allowing the work to relate back to these origins while offering new forms and new meanings. This suggests the possible power of collage practices as tools for inclusive placemaking and design, where a possible future situation would need to account for the complexity and multiplicity of its preceding context.

Collaging existing community narratives, in particular, provides new ways for stakeholders of all kinds to participate in crafting inclusive representations of the language of place. In a collage drawing on stories told by inhabitants and recorded by researchers, a long-time resident's reminiscence of a changing neighbourhood can come into contact with a child's anecdote of a moment of play, a municipal worker's sense of pride in a local project, or a recent arrival's confession of uncertainty about where to make acquaintances with neighbours. These inhabitant-generated narratives could continue to persist in their autonomous forms, even while a collage, whether made by researchers, designers, or the inhabitants themselves, would provide a form of synthesis – an explicitly pluri-vocal text that represents its sources without the risk of subsuming them. Much like any given day in a neighbourhood, in the text of the collage made from community narratives, everyone is talking together.

By traditional definitions, collage would appear to be a strongly non-narrative form, its polyphony seemingly ill-suited to immersive storytelling. It would be difficult to qualify it as anti-narrative, however, and broader understandings of narrative can accommodate collage as a possible form for the complex, multitimbral stories described above. In this way, collage can offer easily accessible tools for representing multiple threads of narrative from typically underrepresented voices in complex urban stories that could not normally be treated within the affordances of the master narratives in top-down planning. Just as anyone with a magazine and scissors can experiment with collage as a visual practice, a textual approach to inclusive collage can start with a piece of paper, a pen, and a question that elicits memories of place.

References

Bakhtin, M. (1984). *Problems of Dostoevsky's Poetics*, translated by Caryl Emerson. Minneapolis, Minnesota: University of Minnesota Press.

Cran, R. (2014). *Collage in Twentieth-Century Art, Literature, and Culture: Joseph Cornell, William Burroughs, Frank O'Hara, and Bob Dylan*. Farnhkam, UK: Ashgate.

Higgins, S. (2019). *Collage and Literature: The Persistence of Vision*. New York and London: Routledge.

Collaging Community Narratives

Assignment

1
Gather residents of a particular neighbourhood and give them loose sheets of paper on which to write.

2
Ask participants to identify a specific memory of a meaningful event from their lives in the neighbourhood/area and to write the story of that moment in that place.

3
Hang the individual memory stories in a space that will allow people to move and read the different texts. Ask participants to circulate and read the memories of the other participants.

4
Ask participants to discuss what they notice about the different memory stories. What surprised them? What felt familiar? What felt like home, even if it wasn't their own memory?

5
During the next phase, the participants select a new theme or prompt, such as, 'We who live here,' or, 'What makes this place?' or another theme of their choice.

6
Ask participants to then compose a new text – a story, a poem, a song, a litany – in which they take small bits of language from every memory story and assemble them together, in whatever order or form they choose, trying to be creative and make something new. (It can help to limit each "snipping" of language to a single phrase, or a certain small number of words, giving structure to the writing and making it easier to include many or even all memory stories.)

7
Allow volunteers to read or perform the new collages to the other participants.

8
Ask participants to discuss the results of the collage. Could they recognize themselves in the texts? How do the collages represent the neighbourhood and its residents? What do the collages say about what it means to live there?

9
(Optional) Have organisers create a final collage drawing from the participants' collages.

10
(Variation) Create a final collage with each participant going back to their original memory story to select their favourite sentence. Arrange the favourite sentences into a new text, at random if time is short. Make an audio recording of the collage with each participant reading their contribution.

Connecting the Nodes

Graph theory to study urban complexity

Jesus Balado Frias
CINTECX, GeoTECH, Universidad de Vigo

In 1736, Leonard Euler solved the Konigsberg seven-bridge problem, which consisted of finding a path that traversed all the bridges by passing over each bridge only once. More important than the answer, was how Euler arrived at the solution. In the bridge problem, topology is a more important feature than geometry. Euler was able to abstract the problem by considering the islands and land masses as nodes and the bridges as the connections between nodes. His solution can be considered as the first example of graph theory.
Today, Konigsberg is called Kaliningrad, the city belongs to Russia and not to Prussia. The bridges are no longer the same, but the solution to the problem is still perfectly valid: it is not possible to traverse all the bridges by passing only once as long as the intermediate nodes of a route have an even number of connections; in other words, there is no solution if there are more than two nodes with an odd number of connections. This approach could be extrapolated to multiple situations – even in relation to urban literature.

Graph theory is an area of mathematics and computer science. Its application reaches social networks, cryptography, blockchain, communications, and computer vision (Majeed & Rauf, 2020). Graph representations are the most abstract way to visualise relations. Graphs have a direct application in urban planning and morphology. The addition of new nodes (areas of interest) and connections are indicative of urban sprawl and complexity. Mobility is a key aspect also reflected in graphs. Urban-network graphs can represent the connections between streets and intersections with the most relevant areas for citizens. Administrative agencies use graphs to promote better connections, more frequent transport, green areas, or security.

According to Pineda Botero, the mapping of urban literature is mostly related to the cartography of physical space and landscape, with concrete mentions of places, monuments, and avenues. But the literary space as the territory evoked by the characters, can be geo-referenced and drawn on a map in relation to urban development and the economic, political, and social contexts (Alves & Queiroz, 2013).

Superimposing the literary space with other layers of information from different sources in the graph will enable the discovery of relations, but also changes to those relations in time. In this way, graph modelling can be useful in the representation of urban scenarios, as graphs allow to reflect the spatial complexity of urban scenarios and may inspire new questions.

References

Alves, D., & Queiroz, A. I. (2013). Studying urban space and literary representations using GIS: Lisbon, Portugal, 1852-2009. *Social Science History*, 37(4), 457-481.

Chen, W.K. (2012). *Applied graph theory* (Vol. 13). Elsevier.

Gross, J.L., & Yellen, J. (2003). *Handbook of graph theory*. CRC press.

Majeed, A., & Rauf, I. (2020). Graph theory: A comprehensive survey about graph theory applications in computer science and social networks. *Inventions*, 5(1), 10.

Wikipedia (2020). List of streets and squares in Königsberg, 1905. url: https://second.wiki/wiki/liste_der_strac39fen_und_plc3a4tze_von_kc3b6nigsberg_1905. Last accessed: 21/01/2022.

Connecting the Nodes

Assignment

1
Select a literary work about a city and get the map of the corresponding area (a screenshot from Google maps is more than enough).

2
Identify the most relevant areas mentioned in the text and place a node in each one. Relevant areas can be exact locations or large areas: squares, gardens, housing, social events, remembered places, districts, streets, avenues, transport stations etc. A useful way to represent the nodes is with a name inside a white circle or a characteristic image.

3
Connect the nodes by lines. Link each node with the nearest nodes based on the character mobility, cultural information, urban cartography, or the relation you consider to be more relevant. Try to not cross the lines and make sure that no node is disconnected. Two nodes can relate to several links to show stronger connections.

4
Add information to each line to improve the understanding of the relations. Relevant information can be distances, route limitations, times, and characters.

5
Indicate on the map: who made the trip, dates, space quality, safety, or flow directions.

6
The map is now generated. You can quickly find out the most relevant places of the literary work and the relations between them. Can you identify events occurred outside the home-range of the characters?

7
Since the writing of the literary work, the urban area may have undergone changes. The graph can be updated accordingly. Have any of the areas changed in a relevant way for the literary work? Would it be possible to follow the same route with the same events today? Does this route correspond to the daily life of the citizens?

assignment

Designing by Participation with Giancarlo de Carlo

method

Ana Rafailovska, Blagoja Bajkovski, Slobodan Velevski
Faculty of Architecture, University Ss Cyril and Methadius

In general, architectural design is understood as a complex process that involves different procedures with concrete aesthetic, functionality, and social effect in the built environment. Frequently however, the former aspects (aesthetics and functionality) of architectural design overshadow the latter one, as Henri Lefebvre remarks: "Too often architecture is designed (and consequently comprehended) as a purely aesthetic or intellectual activity, ignoring social relations and rendering people passive" (Borden, Kerr, Rendell, Pivaro, 2002, p. 5).
On the other hand, participatory design in architecture and urbanism, also known as community design, refers to the involvement of the users in architectural and urban design processes, shifting the paradigm of planning for towards planning with the users (Davidoff, 1965). It embodies extrapolation of various methods that promote balance between the users and the architects, developing new approaches where citizens are given the opportunity to participate in different phases of the design process.

In late 1960s several architects, including Giancarlo de Carlo, Lucien Kroll, Ralph Erskine and others, have introduced a discourse of participatory design in architecture advocating a new approach in designing and comprehending architecture not merely as an expression of designated formal language, but rather as an amalgamated understanding of space with social and cultural content. This proposal takes the process of design of the steelworkers' residential complex *Nuovo Villaggio Matteotti* (1969–1974) in Terni, Italy, by Giancarlo de Carlo as a seminal project on the subject. In this case, the participatory approach reveals architecture as co-creative collaborative act that articulates users' needs within spatial integrity.

The *Matteotti* project transforms architectural design from an authoritarian act into an inclusive process that embodies a set of steps leading to a specific method of participatory design. The method includes four steps:

1 Assembling an interdisciplinary group (architect, architectural historian, engineer, sociologist, and photographer) that mediates between the architect and the steelworkers' families.

Exhibition for a New Villaggio Matteotti, Photo: Mimmo Jodice.

2. Organising an exhibition (Fig.) presenting selected international case studies elaborated through architectural drawings and photographs illustrating residential neighbourhoods aiming to give the future inhabitants a "series of information on ways of living, different from those they have known or experienced so far" (De Carlo, 1969)
3. Conducting interviews with small groups of workers in order to understand their general needs, as basis for conceptual hypotheses of the neighbourhood; and specific needs, as basis for the housing unit's configuration.
4. Preparing preliminary typological schemes represented to the future inhabitants with cardboard models, so that they understand the concepts and decide for their future dwellings.

The aim of these steps is to critically explore, discuss and formulate the socio-spatial framework of the future neighbourhood and the functional layout of preferred lifestyle. The outcome of the process is an integrative architectural design that is informed by collaboration between citizens and professionals.

Nowadays, fifty years after the inception of the Matteotti project, this method has become even more relevant because it introduces interdisciplinary knowledge into the design process and creates neighbourhoods as places of collective endeavour. It is not strictly limited to creating new developments but is equally relevant for adaptive reuse of existing buildings and places, and urban regeneration of whole neighbourhoods.

References

Borden, I., Kerr, J., Rendell, J., Pivaro, A. (2002). *The Unknown City. Contesting Architecture and Social Space*. Cambridge Mass.: The MIT Press.

Davidoff, P. (1965). Advocacy and Pluralism in Planning, *Journal of the American Institute of Planners*, 31, 331-38.

De Carlo, G.; Urbino, Italy; De Seta, C.; Napoli, Italy. (18 December 1969) Personal communication (letter)

Lefebvre, H. (1991). *The Production of Space*, trans. Donald Nicholson-Smith, Oxford: Blackwell.

Further readings

Aravena, A., Iacobelli, A. (2013). *Elemental: Incremental Housing and Participatory Design Manual*. Ostfildern: Hatje Cantz.

Blundell Jones, P., Petrescu, D., Till, J. (2005). *Architecture and Participation*, London and New York: Spon Press.

Charitonidou, M. (2021). Revisiting Giancarlo De Carlo's Participatory Design Approach: From the Representation of Designers to the Representation of Users, *Heritage*, 4(2).

Assignment

1

Assemble an interdisciplinary group of specialists relevant for the project topic, including: an architectural historian/theoretician to provide knowledge regarding the history and the meaning of the place; a sociologist to organise meetings and interviews with the citizens (users, inhabitants); an architect to translate the collected data into an architectural/urban concept; and a photographer to take photos of the designated place/location and the different phases of the design process.

2

Organise thematic events by the members of the interdisciplinary group. This step is an educational and emancipatory phase in the process of design because it informs interested parties with the possibilities for new social and spatial modalities through: Exhibition – a selection of (international) case studies elaborated upon through visual presentations; and lectures – oral presentations of expert knowledge.

3

Interview a representative number of users about their spatial practices in everyday life, their requirements and expectations. The aim of this research phase is to collect material that informs future design. The interview works as a survey that explores and contains general quantitative data but also specific qualitative parameters including functional, social, and cultural information about the place(s) and people involved.

4
Create design schemes, not as a final product, but as a medium representing shared thinking. This last step is part of the participatory design process. It introduces participation through a series of discussions which contribute to the preliminary definition of the social and spatial concept for the future development. The public discussions reinforce the exchange of knowledge in immediate communication between all interested parties and stakeholders.

Double-exposing Place

Analogue photography as a way of shifting perspective

Caendia Wijnbelt
Faculty of Architecture and Landscape Sciences
Leibniz University Hannover

Photographs can keep traces of the ways in which we perceive sites and localities, while at the same time being operative in creating new ways of seeing something we already know intimately. This method explores photography as a mode of inquiry into the lived environment. It highlights features of slowing down and paying attention – often found in analogue processes – that afford shifts in perspective by overlapping and interweaving different environments through experience.

The first image proposed here is an invitation to explore photography – more precisely analogue photography – as a strategy for interpreting the city through the lens of a multilocal experience. It was made in 2017 as part of a research on expectant places, looking into the potential of sites that can seem leftover, overlooked or underused for various reasons. The same roll of film is used twice, once in Haifa and once in Lisbon, producing physical overlays that mimic the way in which both places enter in confluence through the research project. Chance rather than precision is key for this method: the project relies on in-camera chance encounters.

Place, in this practice, is a broad and dynamic term. There is therefore a world of ways in which double-exposing place can evolve. These multilocal dynamics could for example be explored through layering different facets of a single locus. In the example of Lisbon and Haifa (fig.1), two neighbourhoods are explored with a focus on where stillness could be found that leaves room for imagination, and where such stillness could be felt within urban contexts. The results are extremely different in both contexts: one, a forgotten walkway, another, an abandoned in-between floor perched over the city.

The exercise explores how places we have known in the past or in surrounding contexts are very much alive in our minds, and how they can influence our ongoing and new impressions. The superimposition gives weight to two instances of the many experiences through which places are perceived, hinting at the viewers sedimented gaze. As an individual practice, double-exposing place has a broad effect:

Expectant places, Haifa–Lisbon (2016–2018). Photo: Caendia Wijnbelt.

opening an exchange between places, no matter the scale. Through planned and serendipitous ways of layering, each locality set in focus gains unintended meanings that can further be explored.

Double-exposing Place

Assignment

1
First exposures
On your next trip outside of your current city, take a film roll and an analogue camera with you. During your time away, take different photos of your experience in the city: moments with people, buildings and parks. Try to balance scenes without high contrasts between sky and surfaces, focusing on details, textures and snippets of more homogeneously lit places instead, under-exposing slightly.

2
Shifting
After the 36 exposures, rewind the film back into its canister, still in-camera. Be careful not to rewind it all the way, just until you hear the film pop out of the holding mechanism. Once home, open the camera, attach the film again as if it were a new one (in the same position you attached it the first time).

3
Second exposures
Then, start the endeavour of exploring your own neighbourhoods and city, taking photographs of people, locations and events. High contrast scenery and portraits, in this second iteration, are welcomed into the frame, also under exposing them by up to one stop. You may not remember the photos you took in the first exposures: this is part of the choices you have in the planning process, and might be all the more interesting.

4
Impressions
Develop the film, and notice how the two series of experiences in different places overlay. Reflect on these overlays and how they relate. What do they bring out? A first stage of the reflection can focus on capturing these first impressions in writing. Each city or *locus* has specific features which might be reflected in the photographs. The exercise entails relating these. Observing the chance-encounters and what they may bring out is a first lead.

5
Writing
The next stage is about developing these reflections. This task is fragile and the outcomes are uncertain: double exposures are difficult to control despite film's latent capacity to withhold overexposure. Each photographic instance can be explored through a chosen lens. How does architecture encounter its environment? How do two places, or two facets of a place, relate to each other? Which tools can be used to explore the overlaps and differences between them?

6
Outlook
The final stage inquires into the exercise itself, and opens to a new iteration. What would happen if the focuses chosen in each city were reversed (ie. if high contrast portraits were captured while away, and textures were captured at home)? How has the experience of a new place interacted with the city you know well, and how has it perhaps allowed you to view it from another perspective? Finally, which other overlays of place might be interesting to explore?

assignment

Drawing Collectively

Participatory work for depicting the urban environment

Rossella Salerno
Politecnico di Milano

We assume freehand drawing to be a kind of graphic intelligence, the ability to combine the use of the eye, mind, and hand to solve problems and create effective products, aimed at acquiring new knowledge.

The subject of drawing is understood as a transcription or production of thought, a graphic language belonging to the cognitive sphere, and, according to Howard Gardner (1993), as an expression of multiple intelligences, which includes both the experience of space as well as the sphere of visual abilities and manual skills. To draw a place, it is necessary to observe it carefully, almost immersing oneself in it, whereas the photograph, in capturing the scene as a whole, does not require one to have the same mental "attachment" to analyse what a place contains (Treib 2016). Drawing, instead, takes time, attention and knowledge focused on a specific place; drawing requires immersion in a situation, and allows us to verify our observations; drawing within the margins of a sketchpad pushes us to pay more attention, to learn from the page before and to improve on the one after.

Freehand drawing is a type of representation that does not necessarily have to be based on accuracy to convey the conditions of the built environment. Rather, it can be seen as as a tool capable of revealing the relations between the qualities (dimensions, proportions, scale, construction, materials etc.) and lifestyles in urban spaces, so that the analysis of a site, when done well, requires on-site study *accompanied* by the drawing. Drawings can gather both objective information (hard data) – namely dimensions, qualities, geometries, orientation – as well as soft data (experience, use, activities). In general, sketches made on site regard preliminary dimensional analysis for the design or serve as travel notes. 'Sketches in perspective' and 'serial vision' bring together what they observe on route maps and perspective views, similar to how a film builds up sequences rather than capturing single images.

City drawing in this way becomes a series of sketches capable of capturing, in many aspects, the elements the city is made up of. The everyday encounter with the city determines individual differences in how to interpret the urban structure, the effect of use on its form and allows to observe the connection between memory and interpretability: all this falls outside accurate mapping, the main parameter of the urban survey. In short, it is an 'explorative' drawing that demands personal involvement through the visual, phenomenal and atypical aspects of cities, fostering a deeper understanding of the many, disordered but irreplaceable qualities of places.

The aim of collective freehand drawing is to intertwine experience, culture, and vision, realising drawings that transcend what the eye only captures in a single view. Drawing collectively on a scroll brings the participants in touch with the experience of the city. As they work, they start to play off each other, devising other ways of depicting, or better stated, looking and feeling. The stationary point of the drawing has shifts which invites participants to see different objects and relationships than they did in their first position (Dutoit, 2007).

To conduct freehand drawing as collective work, the participants first carry out an individual site visit. They sketch in their notebook the most relevant features in the urban environment and then, as a second step, they reassemble on a paper scroll all drawings they made, producing a collective graphic output. A planning stage is required to choose the most effective views of urban elements. In this way, the individual experiences of place become a shared result by a collective drawing.

References

Dutoit, A., (2007) Looking, inquiring, drawing: the implied urban realm. *Architectural Research Quarterly* Vol. 11 n. 3-4, 311-320.

Gardner, H., (1993). *Multiple Intelligences: The Theory in Practice*. New York: Basic Books.

Treib M. (Eds), (2016). *Drawing/thinking: confronting an electronic age*, London: Routledge, 192.

Drawing Collectively

Assignment

Freehand drawing as collective work: Depicting and Interpreting the urban environment

1
Visit a site to carry out separate freehand drawings in a sketchbook (i.e. views, individual buildings, squares, paths, crossings, walkways etc. but also materials, colours, lights, details, uses etc.).

2
Re-assemble the single sketches on a paper scroll to depict the urban environment as collective work (maximum of 6 people in a group to draw on a paper scroll of 30x180 cm). Expected outcome: intertwined drawings (i.e. plan layout showing paths, visual notes, facades, 3d views etc.) with free compositions and techniques.

3
Depict the experience of urban environment not only by the point of view of a single student but by a shared series of drawings discussed and realised by the whole group. This approach and method allow multifaceted observations to be linked together and so enables the most relevant aspects in an urban place to be highlighted.

Eavesdropping

Overlooked and (over)heard in the city

Alina Cristea
LUCA School of Arts / KU Leuven - the Associated Faculty of the Arts

Navigating a city exposes us not only to its urban space and inhabitants, but also to the fleeting character of their interactions. The double exposure of the images we capture and the sounds we hear in urbanities helps shed a new light on them and their different dynamics. But it also provides an opportunity for reflection on the relationship between image and text. How does one influence the other one?

A way of capturing the ephemeral can be through street photography, freezing the decisive moment in a photograph like Cartier-Bresson (1952), but eavesdropping and writing down overheard conversations or recollecting one's own interactions with people in the public space is also able to achieve that. Their association can help complete the image of a city and can contribute to finding patterns, possible stereotypes, and common concerns of its city dwellers. The public transport, local markets, the supermarket and public institutions, like the post office, the city hall or museums, can function as public forums for people voicing their frustrations and their actual opinions in an uncensored manner about the places they inhabit. The spontaneous nature of overheard speech, and the fact that speakers assume no one is listening to their conversation provides veracity to what they are telling, and consequently provides greater insight into the psychology of urban spaces; even more so than through interviews or questionnaires trying to capture the vox pop in a more controlled and edited way.

Some encounters with overheard speech are very brief and can be fragmented, like when you overhear snippets of a conversation or just one sentence, when people are passing you by on the street. But one overheard sentence or joke can synthesize an entire public opinion on a current matter. Therefore, it can provide an insightful look into a city or a way of capturing local humour. "Humour has long formed as valid a part of the lexicon of street photography as more earnest social documentary" (Howarth and McLaren, 2010). Much like a street photographer, the observer or eavesdropper must rely on his/her agility of the mind and the tools they have at their disposal to 'record' the overheard happenings. It could be a notebook, your smartphone, a keyword written on a small piece of napkin that would later help you recollect what you have heard. Some conversations 'find' you, when you just happen to be at the right place at the right time and pay attention to your environment and the people around you. But at times you must be proactive about it and look for the right spot or sit in the proximity of people who seem interesting to you or who are already engaged in a conversation. Great catalysers of impromptu conversation are the public transport and markets. You could take an afternoon to ride a bus or a tram from one end to the other and listen to what people around you are saying. If you are (un) lucky you might even witness a public scandal.

One challenge of this method is the necessity to speak or at least understand the local language(s). The absence of this prerequisite might contribute more to the comic, humorous part of this exercise, but would make the recollection of the encounter and the findings less reliable.

Similar practices relying on the systematic collection and archiving of overheard conversations were made in New York, Dublin, Bucharest and finally, 'Everywhere' on dedicated web pages – at first, on websites and blogs, then followed by Facebook, Twitter, and Instagram pages. These are mostly initiated and maintained by locals of these places with the help of the community who is contributing their stories, often illustrated by a third person (generally, a cartoonist or illustrator) that wasn't the initial 'eavesdropper'. Contemporary anecdotes, unintended wisdom or local jokes help (re)create the image of our own cities or of the ones we only know from the media, and are, therefore, great source material for identifying and creating new narratives of cities.

References
Cartier-Bresson, H. (1952). *The Decisive Moment*. New York: Simon & Schuster.

Howarth, S., & McLaren, S. (2010). *Street photography now*. London: Thames & Hudson.

Examples/Applications
The New Yorker. Overheard in New York Sketchbook. www.newyorker.com/humor/sketchbook/overheard-in-new-york. Accessed 13 Apr. 2022.

Further readings
Hegarty, S. (2005, August 20th). *Eavesdropping on everyday chat*. The Irish Times. http://www.irishtimes.com/news/eavesdropping-on-everyday-chat-1.482642.

Zoller Seitz, M. (2018, February 5th). *Overheard lives: an appreciation of eavesdropping in the city*. Ebert Digital LLC. http://www.rogerebert.com/mzs/overheard-lives-an-appreciate-of-eavesdropping-in-the-city.

Eavesdropping

Assignment

1
Take the public transport (bus, tram, or metro; the trolleybus offers even more opportunities because it takes you slower through the city) in your city/neighbourhood. If necessary, stay on until the last stop or ride it from one end to the other.

2
Pay attention to your surroundings and let serendipity happen to you. Just make sure you have something with you so you can write it down when it does happen – e.g. your phone, your notebook, or make a mental note of it until you can put it down on paper.

3
If you are going to use the overheard information, make sure that it is not possible to later link it to the person who said it. Don't take photos or make recordings of them.

4
Take a photograph or make a drawing that has a link with the story and that helps place it in a wider context without the image becoming just an illustration of the text. What are the new text-image relations created this way? Can the two media (text and image) still function individually?

5
Now try the same thing on a park bench. You could sit in the comfortable proximity of people who are already engaged in a conversation that strikes your interest. Or while you are sitting by yourself on a bench, you might find that other passers-by will sit nearby. (optional)

6
You could also try it while waiting in a queue at your local supermarket or at a local public institution. There are no better places to overhear conversations or hear people voicing their frustrations than in places where they are waiting for something. (optional)

7
How did the focus on conversations make you experience the urban public space? Did you notice or experience something unexpected?

assignment

Engaging (with) Images
Place-based future stories

Panu Lehtovuori
School of Architecture, Tampere University

The aim of this method is to allow citizens, regardless of their age, social context and working background, to imagine collectively meaningful place-based stories looking to the future. Engaging (with) Images is useful in a broad variety of situations; from mapping local knowledge to idea-generation, and from participatory urban planning to conflict resolution.

To make *Engaging (with) Images* work, you first need a set of image-cards, second, a map of the study area, and third, a group of participants. The set of image-cards is the most unique element of this method. You need a rather big number of different images, in the range of 50-100, or even more. Their content should be varied: images from the site, images related in direct and indirect ways to the theme or question of the meeting, as well as evocative examples from other cities and contexts. Ideally, there should be both long views and close-ups, both crowded spaces and empty vistas, both winter and summer. Besides urban situations, the selection of images should include objects (for example a tree, a car, a phone, a ruin, or a toy), as well as pure materials and colours. Very importantly, there should also be abstract cards: arrows, mathematical signs, and other symbols.

Depending on the number of participants, the organiser should provide 3-5 copies of each card for people to choose. So the total number of printed cards is 200-500. The cards can be in postcard format or a bit smaller, as rectangles or squares. It is essential to print on thick paper or cardboard so that the cards are easy to handle. The original source of the images is free, as far as the organiser has the right to use them. Good sources are the organisers' own pictures, Creative Commons licensed images and other public images, for example local museum's collections. Architecture magazines, tourism brochures and local press may also be used, but in these cases permissions for use have to be requested.

The map is important for participants to locate their story. Its graphic quality may vary, but it is important to keep it readable and understandable. As such, a typical municipal address map or an Open Street Map is often better than the technical maps used in profes-

Eteläpuisto cards. Two participants' visual narratives of the future of Eteläpuisto, the South Park in the city of Tampere, Finland. Credits: Panu Lehtovuori & Markus Laine.

sional planning and urban design. While the map's size should be adapted to the situation, it would be ideal to have a large table-top map for people to gather around, work with the image-cards, and discuss. On this map-table, the participants position their image-stories.

The participants of *Engaging (with) Images* are asked to explore the images, choose four (or 3-5) of them, and order them to represent a story of a desirable future situation on the site. Because of the relatively big number of images on the map-table, it is important to give enough time to work; half an hour at least. Often, people want to chat and change ideas, compare their choices, laugh and enjoy the situation. Coffee and snacks help a lot. After the selection and socializing talks, each participant is asked to tell the story. An additional note: in some cases, it may be important to visit the site together before working with the image-cards.

Together, the visual narratives create a playful canvas of ideas on the map. This method helps participants to move away from static ideas, towards viewing the future as dynamic and relational. In many cases it is enough to document the result of the participatory moment by recording and photographing. To deepen the work, it is also possible to count which images were most popular, and proceed towards a qualitative interpretation of the connotations of participants' choices. This option is especially relevant if you want to engage different user groups in a series of *Engaging (with) Images* meetings. In the city of Narva in Eastern Estonia, our SPIN Unit team, collaborating with Linnalabor, engaged youth groups to discuss the city's future and their aspirations. After the participatory sessions, we produced a graphically powerful poster of youths' future vision for Narva.

Further reading
www.spinunit.org

Assignment

1
Choose a relevant site for discussing and imagining its future (after the implementation of a urban renewal, a heritage preservation site, or a culture-led development) through the angle of a topical theme. The site can be a neighbourhood, a street or a square, an urban block, or a singular building. Examples might range from free spaces for youth, to contemporary social housing, or from enabling urban activism to increasing biodiversity. Urban conflicts are also possible topics here.

2
Start making the set of image-cards by making a tentative selection of 50 pictures, with views from the site, ideas and pictures from elsewhere, images linked to the theme, and abstract pictures, such as mathematical symbols. Use your own images and public ones, such as Creative Commons licensed images.

3
Assemble the images in order to create a story of the future of the site according to the chosen theme.

4
Explain the story to at least three colleagues, friends or local residents. In that group, develop the picture selection, adding new ideas and dimensions to the story, as well as new image sources, for example the local museum collection or other's own or family pictures.

5
Finalise the images with Photoshop filters to intended print size (eg. 10 x 15 cm), resolution (eg. 200 dpi) and colour profile. Congratulations, you now have the set of image-cards, the most unique element of Engaging (with) Images, ready in your hard drive, waiting to be used in a participatory situation!

6
Use your contacts to organise the Engaging (with) Images event or series of events with a map-table of the site and snacks to help socializing. Groups of not more than 10 participants are recommended for everyone to be active and heard.

7
Invite the participants to make their personal future stories with images. Discuss the stories and the places they relate to, giving voice to every participant. Make notes and photograph the situation.

8
After the first event (or a piloting series of events), reflect carefully and critically on the set of image-cards and your documentation of the discussions. Which images were chosen by the participants, and why? How did people comment on the images? Are some themes or dimensions

missing? Do you see unnecessary repetition? Based on the reflection, improve your set – which becomes a valuable asset for you and your team, thinking towards future Engaging (with) Images events.

assignment

Exhausting Urban Places
...à *la* Georges Perec

method

Jeremy Allan Hawkins
École Nationale Supérieure d'Architecture de Strasbourg

In 1974, Georges Perec sat down at a café in Place Saint-Sulpice in Paris and turned his attention to "the rest": not heritage buildings, not seats of municipal power, not local hotspots or critical infrastructure. The Oulipian writer considered that the landmarks of such a Parisian square had already been catalogued and described countless times; he wanted to instead consider the seemingly unimportant, the overlooked and the trivial. Writing over three consecutive days, Perec produced what was later published as *Tentative d´épuisement d´un lieu parisien* (1982) (An Attempt at Exhausting a Place in Paris).

In his experiment, Perec makes lists, asks questions, registers uncertainties in parentheses, and records urban phenomena as they enter his consciousness. In so doing, he offers readers an inventory of, "some strictly visible things," dealing, for example, with the raw text of local signage – a "P" stands for parking *t/here*, while the initials, "KLM," advertise an airborne voyage *elsewhere* – or noting down the movements of passing dog walkers and baby strollers. His attention to detail not only collects but also signifies, transforming a vague sense of the life of the city into a concrete and specific index. What exactly does a rainy Sunday *mean* for Saint-Sulpice in 1974? Fewer buses and more private vehicles, for one, and people struggling to protect cakes from the elements, for another.

Perec also manages to capture a certain notion of urban rhythm, without explicitly arguing for it. The steady and repeated passing of buses, for example, forms a temporal beat in the text (made more apparent in the moments in which he loses interest in them and stops recording), and yet we might understand the rhythm of the place to be linked as much to the bus schedule as to the qualitative events that transpire between those intervals: a child carrying groceries, a conversation between two retirees, an explosion of pigeons into the air, or a policeman pacing as he reads in the square. Each minor event serves as a kind of micro-narrative, an invitation to imagination and story, where a girl with a blue balloon becomes the protagonist (of the text, of the city) for the length of a phrase.

In the end, we could argue that his attempt exhausted Perec as much as the place itself. He sits at a table, moves to a public bench, decides to go upstairs at the café to eat, and returns to the table he occupied before. Over time, he starts to express fatigue, discomfort, hunger and thirst, and complains of "unsatisfied curiosity" as he tries to track the subtle differences between one day and the next at Saint-Sulpice. Throughout the experiment, the author is present as an attention, a perspective, a situated eye/I, but occasional bursts of ego reveal an embodied quest to find a new strategy for understanding the city: 'How to see the fabric if only the rips are visible?' Perec wonders.

The response would be, it seems from the text, to force oneself. Or to put in place a method in which we are obliged to sit and attend to minutiae that we ignore in daily life – the very opposite of Sartre's example of the moment in which, in pure non-reflection, we run to catch the tram. Perec, rather, turns to deliberate conscious attention, and the result offers a unique urban score; telling of the character and quality of life in the French capital and around a particular city square, including the moments in which it leaves him cold and dispirited. By taking cues from Perec's experiment, we can start to grasp both the abundance of urban phenomena waiting to be noticed, but also come more fully into our embodied experience of them when the initial excitement starts to wear off.

References

Perec. G. (1982). *Tentative d'épuisement d'un lieu parisien*. Paris: Christian Bourgois.

Perec, G. (2010). *An Attempt at Exhausting a Parisian Place*, translated by Marc Lowenthal. Cambridge, Mass.: Wakefield Press.

Sartre, J.P. (1988/2004). *The Transcendence of the Ego: A Sketch for a Phenomenological Description*, translated by Andrew Brown. London and New York: Routledge.

Further Reading

Cooper, D. (2017, November 2). *Spotlight on…Georges Perec An Attempt at Exhausting a Place in Paris* (1975). DC's. https://denniscooperblog.com/spotlight-on-georges-perec-an-attempt-at-exhausting-a-place-in-paris-1975-2/

Mott, W. (1984). *Poetics of Experiment: A Study of the World of Georges Perec*. Lexington, Kentucky: French Forum.

Examples

Crowe, M. (2017). *An Attempt at Exhausting a Place*. In GTA Online. Studio Operative.

Exhausting Urban Places

Assignment

1
Choose an urban location in which to spend an extended period of time – an afternoon, a full day, or even three. Select an exact starting position in the space which allows you to observe and take notes. This can be a bench, a café, or even on the ground if you wish, as long as you are able to write.

2
Start by noting the date, the time, the place, your exact location, and the weather.

3
Create an inventory of visible language, writing down all that you can see from your vantage point: signs, posters, slogans, symbols, t-shirts, license plates, etc.

4
When you have exhausted the visible language as much as you can (stand), start a new inventory of things: vehicles, furniture, materials, vegetation, and other objects.

5
When the inventories of visible language and things begin to feel complete, shift your attention to and note down all the small or individual movements and events: pieces and parts of infrastructure, people moving, public transport passing by, urban wildlife and its behaviour.

6
When you feel like you are no longer seeing anything new, turn your attention to sound, describing the soundscape and trying to capture overheard bits of conversation.

7
Periodically – once an hour, for example – observe and record how you are feeling, in your body and in your mood.

8
Repeat steps 3-7 throughout the time period you set for yourself. Don't be afraid to move to another position later, if a new perspective on the place will help keep the exercise going.

9
At the end of the observation, look back over your text. What kinds of things caught your attention? Do you find any patterns or relationships? What is revealed about the life of the place that might be hidden behind obvious landmarks? How did your feelings change through the exercise?

assignment

Framing the City in Words and Images

The visual urban essay

Luc Pauwels
Department of Communication Studies, University of Antwerp

Visual scholarly-communication products comprise a broad variety of ways to visualise and express insights in novel, more experimental and experiential ways. They include rich traditions such as social scientific filmmaking and the approach of the visual essay (Grady, 1991), as well as emerging communicative phenomena such as digital storytelling, photo-novellas, and more arts-based approaches such as exhibitions, performances, and art installations.

The images of a visual essay are often being made with this final purpose in mind, so that they will be more apt to fulfil their expressive role, both through what they depict (subject matter) and how they depict it (formal traits).

Today the term 'visual essay' is used for a variety of formats which have moved far beyond the paper-based pictures and text combinations or linear short movies. They vary in length and breadth from concise articles to book length contributions, from short clips to full length films on DVD or the web, from poster size compositions to room-filling exhibitions and art installations.

In principle, a visual essay may consist of any type of static or moving visual or multimodal representation. It can make use of pre-existing images or images explicitly produced for the purpose, and they may be of either photographic or non-photographic (drawings, paintings, graphics) nature.

Boosted by new media technologies and networking opportunities, the visual essay has developed into a contemporary vehicle for voicing and visualising all sorts of personal reflections, new ideas, arguments, experiences, and observations, thereby taking any possible hybrid variation and combination of a manifesto, critical review, testimony or just a compelling story.

The major challenge and strength of this scholarly form resides in the skilful production and synergetic combination of visual

Picture originally titled 'The Urban Panopticon / Los Angeles', and taken from 'Street Discourse: A Visual Essay on Urban Signification' (Pauwels, 2009). This photo essay attempts to interrogate and confront the multi-authored communicative spaces of cities through a combination of evocative texts and purposefully made pictures from actual aspects of urban material culture and human behaviour. Both the textual and the visual parts of this essay conjure a view on the city as an extremely hybrid semiotic space – a huge, out of control combination of interventions made by actors, with different, often conflicting interests. The visual essay implicitly and metaphorically examines these multiple intermeshing discourses – the historic, the political, the social, the communicative, the multicultural, the commercial, the religious etc. – which provide the city with its unpredictable, multi-layered, and never fully graspable character.

materials with other signifiers – words, layout and design – adding up to a scientifically informed statement. The visual essay occupies a particular place in research practice, balancing between art and science, information and expression. Its particular strengths are its broad expressive range; its 'open-ended', polysemic, and multi-vocal character; its hybrid multi-media or multi modal and cross-platform appearance; and its largely uncodified nature. These are simultaneously its greatest challenges and a potential source of controversy ('is it art or science?') (Pauwels, 2012; 2015). The visual 'urban' essay takes aspects of life in the city, both visible behaviour and material culture, as its prime subject. It is a way to communicate insights and experiences rather than a systematic method for producing visual data. It usually requires an extended period of prior research before the visuals and texts match up to produce an expressive whole.

References

Pauwels, L. (2012). Conceptualizing the 'visual essay' as a way of generating and imparting sociological insight: Issues, formats and realisations. *Sociological Research Online*, 17(1).

Pauwels, L. (2015). *Reframing Visual Social Science: Towards a More Visual Sociology and Anthropology*. Cambridge University Press.

Grady, J. (1991). The Visual Essay and Sociology, *Visual Sociology*, 6(2), 23-38.

Examples/Applications

Gómez Cruz, E. (2020). Black screens: a visual essay on mobile screens in the city. *Visual Communication*, 19 (1), 143-156.

Pauwels, L. (2009). Street Discourse: A Visual Essay on Urban Signification. *Culture Unbound*, 1, 263-272.

Sullivan, E. & Ledesma, E. (2015). Same trailer, different park. *Contexts*, 14(1), 50-57.

Assignment

1
Explore the city for days in a row while producing photographs of what seems noteworthy to you.

2
Gradually develop an idea (a verbal and visual argument) for addressing a particular aspect or issue of that city.

3
Write an evocative text (or poem) to go with the images (introductory text and/or captions).

4
Organise the textual and visual parts into an expressive whole (Carefully thinking about a title, appropriate typography, layout, and with certain publication options in mind).

5
Ask a number of respondents to look at your visual essay and note down their reactions and comments. Use these to fine-tune your verbal and visual argument (e.g. more or other captions, revisit the order of the images, make the text more evocative, and so forth).

assignment

Geotagging the Urban Landscape

Data harvest through social media

Eleni Oureilidou and Konstantinos Ioannidis
School of Architecture, Aristotle University of Thessaloniki

In the post-digital landscape, geotagging is suggested as a tool to read the landscape as a text and to enrich the semantic layer of urban space. This is based on the writings of Ian Hay, which state that visual objects or written texts would provide insights into effects and carry articulated meanings about social conditions (Hay, 2016). Furthermore, the appropriation of urban open spaces and meaning-making mechanisms are studied here under the scope of a dialectic between landscape architecture, programming, and technology (Hudson-Smith, 2007). In that sense, geotagging becomes a part of digital narrativity for the labelling of site-specific data and enables the matching of places with stories. In turn, it reveals collective reflections towards urban landscapes and places or elements that draw the immediate attention of the landscape's onlookers. This process also involves the sharing, layering through resharing, and networking of site-specific information, and it is suggested to increase the spatial capacity of urban spaces. In that context, the tool of geotagging would raise awareness about various social issues, such as the visibility and segregation of displaced people, based on various perspectives and stories.

In this regard, the process of geotagging would involve concepts and categories of narrativity to "read" or understand city centres as arrival hubs and contested terrains. The research method proposes the examination of novel applications and methodologies that would incorporate the tool of geo-tagging and its semantic significations. This includes the Visual Ethnography, as introduced by Sarah Pink (2012), and 'Ethnocomputation' (Tedre et al., 2006). Based on that, big data landscapes and social media platforms enable new differentiated structures and models for the representation of information, opening new ways of manipulating organised information, such as the recommendation algorithms.

Towards that direction, the users' data about landscape appropriation are collected from different social media channels, including media posts from Twitter accounts of collectives or images retrieved from Instagram accounts. These narrative artefacts would suggest specific locations and tags to mediate different assemblages of everyday life in each context. In addition, the retrieved data would offer an understanding of stances and social routines, as well as the dynamics in the scale of the neighbourhood, the park, or the street. In the context of this research, everyday data collection and implementation goes further to incorporate a prototype digital storytelling platform as an interactive interface to facilitate the semantics of landscape through geotagging. This website would include different portals, where users can share their stories linking them with urban spaces, denoting urban characteristics and concepts linked to their landing or settlement. Moreover, users could get information about collectives, create, and join groups or organize events online and in physical places, producing visual materials to promote their speech.

Ultimately, based on the visual analysis of geotagged information and the consideration of selected artefacts as texts, different categories of narrativity, concepts and uses of urban spaces would emerge. The new concepts would frame a social "sense of place", inform about place-making and landscape appropriation, and acknowledge geotagging as a medium for communities to restore self-organised communal domains in new lands. A further implementation of this tool would incorporate routes based on georeferenced data to link urban spaces in arrival neighbourhoods and label them accordingly to match spatial concepts with narrative aspects.

References

Hay, I. (2016). *Qualitative Research Methods in Human Geography*. Oxford University Press.

Hudson-Smith, A. (2007). *Digital Urban - The Visual City* (CASA Working Paper Series 124). Centre for Advanced Spatial Analysis: London.

Martínez Diez, P., Santamaria Varas, M., & Bari Corberó, J. (2016). atNight designing the city at night. http://www.atnight.ws

Pink, S. (2012). *Doing Visual Ethnography* (Second Edition). SAGE Publications Ltd.

Tedre, M., Sutinen, E., Kahkonen, E., & Kommers, P. (2006). Ethnocomputing: ICT in cultural and social context. *Communications of the ACM*, 49(1), 126–131.

Geotagging the Urban Landscape

Assignment

1
Identify online social spaces that accommodate media posts from collectives or individuals acting or walking in the neighbourhood. These would include social media platforms like Twitter and Instagram.

2
Collect data from a sample of stories concerning specific urban places in the form of geotagging to inform about recurrent activities like manifestations, or cultural activities.

3
Categorise data based on different concepts to signify semantically different urban places.

4
Create a website as an interactive interface that would link stories with places based on geotagging and data analysis of social media channels. Which urban spaces emerge based on social media platforms and which concepts describe them? Are the concepts and urban spaces retrieved from Instagram and Twitter the same? Which urban spaces are reflected in stories posted in the portals and forums of the website? Which could be the concepts that would describe them, are they different or the same as the social media channels?

5
Recommend new georeferenced tags based on the emergence of concepts to suggest routes in the neighbourhood for displaced populations.

assignment

Horizontal-viewing

method

Menatulla Hendawy
Interdisciplinary Urban Planner, Technical University Berlin

Urban planners, urban designers, and architects are systematically educated to look at cities and buildings from a birds-eye view. 'Horizontal-city-viewing' could be a method of seeing and understanding everyday spatial realities from a more grounded perspective. It can help in upgrading the planners' and architects' understanding of the local city relationships amongst themselves, as well as in their communications with the general public. It can also allow for ground-up reflections of global urban dynamics that are contextualised and situated in the lived spatial realities. It is about experiencing the city to understand it and to reflect on it. This can be viewed as an on-site experiment that is consciously changing.

Viewing the city horizontally is especially relevant, considering that urban planning is viewed as a field that addresses so-called 'wicked problems,' a term coined by Rittel and Webber (1973). Viewing the city horizontally can help to deconstruct the complexity of cities and the multiple, unpredictable issues in a simple way: by seeing the city from below. In a similar vein, de Certeau (1984) compares the view from above (from Manhattan's world trade centre) with the view from the walkers of the city, basing his critique on what he calls the "concept city," arguing for a view from below, that takes into account what he calls "the ordinary practitioners of the city." (De Certeau, 1984, p.93) Extending de Certeau's conception, Viewing the city horizontally is about the angle of seeing and experiencing the city by walkers as well as other city wanderers. Horizontal viewers see, and live in spaces that are accordingly co-constructed. Viewing the city horizontally constitutes a significant way of seeing the city that can help in not only describing and narrating contemporary cities, but also with critically reflecting on them. This view can allow us to notice and experience the effects of global urban trends such as the non-linearisation of urban spaces or the creation of walls to control urban movement.

The instruments that can be used in Horizontal-city-viewing can include real time note taking and photographing of the city. For more interaction, speak with those people one meets during a Horizontal-city-viewing experiment. One of the approaches to Horizontal-city-viewing could be (critical) visual methodologies. However, more experiments are needed to understand and expand the possibilities of viewing the city horizontally. The outcomes of a method are free to emerge accordingly. Analysis of outcomes of such an experiment (i.e. photos or notes) describing how a city is actually seen – horizontally – can illustrate for us the grounded, lived, and everyday experiences of living in the city. In turn, this can teach us about everyday city encounters in relation to a variety of aspects such as urban, social, environmental, economic, mental, behavioural, cognitive, and human spatial phenomena.

References
De Certeau, M. (1984). *The Practice of Everyday Life*. Berkeley: University of California Press.

Rittel, H. W., & Webber, M.M. (1973). Dilemmas in a general theory of planning. *Policy sciences*, 4(2), 155-169.

Further Reading
Hendawy, M., (2022). *Spatio-Visual Co-constructions: Communication and Digitalization of Urban planning in a mediatized world, Cairo as a glocal case*. Phd Thesis. TU Berlin.

Hendawy, M. and Saeed, A., (2019). "Beauty and the Beast: The Ordinary City versus the Mediatised City – The Case of Cairo". *Urbanisation*, 4(2), 126-134.

Horizontal-viewing

Assignment

1
Define your eye level, don't look up or down. Only make photos of anything (for example, this can be a route, a public space etc.) that appears at eye level.

2
Decide on the sequence of understanding the field (for example, if you decided in Step 1 to view a route, decide on the direction of viewing; if you decide on viewing a public space where multiple social activities come together, such as a market square or a street crossing, plan to turn 360 degrees and make a panorama on eye level).

3
Decide on the method or instruments you will use to document this field (i.e. photos, notes).

4
Select from your panorama or photo sequence several everyday encounters and describe them in detail.

5
Look at the materials and spend some time reflecting on them: What was your first impression looking at and living in the field horizontally? What did you see, notice, and feel? What does this tell you about what you were looking for? Do you have other insights?

6
Close the circle, reflect back at Step 1 and challenge those who would follow your steps to see horizontally.

assignment

Imagining Dialogues with the Voiceless

method

Saskia de Wit
Section of Landscape Architecture, Delft University of Technology

An imaginary dialogue is a classical literary device to give a voice to those who cannot speak for themselves. Plato and Lucian already recorded imaginary dialogues centuries ago between famous protagonists of differing views as a literary form of argumentative conversation - arguing, urging, agreeing, or staking out contradictions. Their protagonists were voiceless since they were long dead. Likewise, an imaginary dialogue can be used to give a voice to those components of the city that remain hidden to us because we don't speak the same language. We tend to think of cities as human communities in relation to their physical surroundings. But these surroundings are built up of characters and creatures that are also inhabiting the city; our cities are multi-species habitats, that we share with innumerable other-than-human beings. Philosopher and sociologist Bruno Latour (1993) developed the idea that the separation between nature and culture is an illusion, and that non-human actors should have the same rights as humans. If we begin to understand non-humans as protagonists, as fellow citizens with their own rights and their own perceptions, we can gain a deeper understanding of the cities that we live in.

An imaginary dialogue is a device that can aid in such an understanding of non-humans as fellow citizens, giving them a voice. Such a dialogue can take the form of an interview, in which you are the interviewer. The aim of an interview is to gain insight in the perspective of others, and to extract information about a certain topic from a protagonist who has knowledge about this topic - because of their expertise or experience. When an interview is open-ended and cyclically-iterative, determined by the interviewer as much as by the interviewee, it becomes a dialogue. The twentieth century Russian philosopher and literary theorist Mikhail Bakhtin (1986), described the concept of the dialogue as being:

> ...the single adequate form for verbally expressing authentic human life. [In it] a person participates wholly and throughout his whole life: with his eyes, lips, hands, soul, spirit, with his whole body and deeds. Dialogic relations have a specific nature: they can be reduced neither to the purely logical (even if dialectical) nor to the purely linguistic (compositional-syntactic)... Where there is no word

> *and no language, there can be no dialogic relations; they cannot exist among objects or logical quantities (concepts, judgments, and so forth). Dialogic relations presuppose a language. (p. 117)*

How can we converse with those that do not speak our language? "How do you give a voice to a Thing, Plant or Animal? What does the Water tell us and what choices does the Iron make?" (The Parliament of Things, n.d.) We cannot know how others than ourselves perceive the world. So, to give them a voice and treat them with respect and seriousness, as an equal, you need background research. Paradoxically, at the same time we need to be very much aware that we can only see things from our own perspective: the perspective of the interviewer. From that perspective, from your own relation to the subject, you can observe the subject so close that you can put yourself in their shoes, so to speak, immerse yourself in them, as architectural historian Erik de Jong paraphrased the Greek philosopher Heraclitus: "to understand something about water, you have to actually stand in it." (2020)

An interview needs both preparation and expression. The dialogue stands at the centre of preceding research and notation afterwards. Observe your subject as an individual, precisely and from different angles. How does it look, smell, sound? How is the relation between its details and its overall form? How is it different from its relatives? How does it respond to changing conditions? With the aim of a dialogue, you will look at your subject with different eyes. The notation of the interview also determines the knowledge you will retrieve. It might be poem, a short story, a script, or a film. The best form is not a fixed format but will be determined between you and your interviewee.

References

Bakhtin, M. M. (1986). *Speech Genres and Other Late Essays*. Trans. by Vern W. McGee. Austin, Tx: University of Texas Press.

Jong, E. de (2020). Lecture The tree that owns itself, or: new thoughts on the relationship between humans and non-humans. Brightspace: https://brightspace.tudelft.nl

Latour, B. (1993). *We have never been modern*. Trans. by Catherine Porter. Cambridge, Mass.: Harvard University Press.

The Parliament of Things (n.d.). Retrieved 03 February 2020, from https://theparliamentofthings.org

Assignment

1

Select a single tree. Get to know your interviewee intimately. This you do by literally approaching it from different directions. Determine the cardinal directions.

2

Firstly, experience and document the characteristics of the east side of the chosen specimen tree by close observation. Start from as far away as possible (e.g. the other side of the street, or building façade) to get a full view of the tree from top to bottom. Take note of the tree's dimensions (shape, height and width of crown and trunk), branch structure, transparency.

3

Next, move to c. 1,5 metre from the tree. Use each of your senses: register the movement of leaves, sounds, changes in shade pattern on the ground, insects and birds or the traces they left behind, etc.

4

Document your experiences in overall as well as close-up photos and drawings: showing microscale patterns, colours, forms, structures, as well as descriptions, associative words, sound recordings, film, etc.

5

Repeat steps 2-4 for the south, west and north side. Pay attention to the differences with the east side: the overall shape (no tree is symmetrical), the different temperature and amount of moss growing on the trunk, etc.

6

Now, imagine you are the tree: stand or sit with your back against the tree and observe the surroundings. Move around tree, and project your senses outward: look, listen, feel the soil, feel the air. Touch the trunk with your hands, look closely at a leaf. Look up from the base of the trunk, feel and look at the texture of the trunk, branches, leaves, the temperature of the trunk, the pattern of the roots, smell, marks left by people or cars, etc.

7

Now you know enough about your subject to interview the tree: how might the urban environment be perceived from the perspective of the tree? The next steps you might either do on site or behind your desk. Create a conversation by jumping between the recorded perceptions toward and from the tree. What can the tree tell you about the surrounding urban landscape that would otherwise escape your attention? What would it see or hear if it had eyes or ears? How do the surroundings affect the tree (shade from buildings, suffocation from paving, damage from parked bikes, etc.)?

assignment

8
Imagine what it might have witnessed from the moment it was planted here until now. Think about both progressive and cyclical changes. Does it have any opinions about the changes it witnessed? How do these changes affect the tree?

9
How does it interact with its surroundings? What other species live in and around the tree, both above and below ground? How do they communicate?

10
Devise your own notation system for the fictional interview, options include: classical interview text, short story, poem, drawing, immersive film, etc. Use your findings from steps 2-6 to support the story.

method

Intervening Tactically

Urban action research

Mattias Malk
Estonian Academy of Arts, Tallinn

Small scale, low budget, DIY, provisional, informal, insurgent, vernacular, guerrilla, tactical, open-source: these are a few of the labels given to a particular kind of city making. This approach has been spreading throughout the world for a while, but tends to proliferate in times of crises and in response to a lack of resources. Their common denominator is citizen-led improvement. They are also united in a spirit of, 'mess around and find out,' which has significant potential for developing a more participatory kind of urban observation and research practice. In other words, one way to learn about the urban environment is to become an active participant in its creation.

For example, after initial observations and interviews or eliciting local knowledge through more participative methods, a researcher could design a tactical urban intervention in response to their findings. In workshops with students these have taken various surprising forms. For one, in the shape of public events such as a concert in a disused venue, a block party, or the act of collaboratively cleaning up a public space. In other cases, physical installations on site have been made such as benches, posters with oral histories, improved signage for cyclists, or even an improvised golf course.

The aim of such interventions can be to prototype a design hypothesis. This could be valuable for architects, planners, or citizen initiatives. However, the more general aim is to create a double-loop of learning, whereby the intervention in the social and physical makeup of the urban environment creates a new condition to observe and feeds back into further research. Moreover, this methodology is highly iterative and can be repeated after reflection. However, as this method is typically labour intensive, it is better suited for group projects. The researcher can also choose the role of facilitator instead of maker and enable respondents to design their own interventions.

This approach could be defined as 'tactical urban action research' and exists somewhere between the concept of the spectacle devised by the Situationist International, and the practice of tactical urbanism. This means that the action taken should neither be purely

Intervening stickers - student project about lacking spatial quality in public transport waiting areas.

critical nor solutionist. Instead, the researcher must adopt a sense of good will and experimentation. Even a strategic sense of naivety and vulnerability would be useful, especially when working in an unfamiliar context or with marginalised respondents. By also employing tact and social responsibility, this method of practical research can be a valuable way to test assumptions and situate a research project.

This methodology involves direct intervention and impacts the local environment. Therefore, it is crucial to not spoil the field! Act responsibly, admit mistakes and be prepared to explain your intentions. Is your intervention permanent? When is the experiment over and what happens after? Furthermore, since you are dealing with people and interfering in the environment, it is vital to acknowledge that reporting back is part of exiting the field. At the very least share your findings with your respondents in a personal setting. If your intervention was larger in nature or yielded valuable information, you should also consider publishing your findings via local or social media.

Intervening Tactically

Further readings
Goodnough, K. (2008). Dealing with Messiness and Uncertainty in Practitioner Research: The Nature of Participatory Action Research. *Canadian Journal of Education*. 31(2), 431-458.

Ku, H.B., & Kwok, J. Y. (2015). The action research practice of urban planning - An example from Hong Kong. In H. Bradbury, *The SAGE handbook of action research* London: SAGE, 118-130.

Mould, O. (2014). Tactical Urbanism: The New Vernacular of the Creative City. *Geography Compass*, 8(8), 529–539.

Shepard, C. (2017). *Citymakers: The culture and craft of practical urbanism*. Monacelli Press, LCC.

Examples
Spacemakers (2013). Cricklewood Town Square.

Linnalabor & Noblessner quarter (2016). Tallinn beta-promenade.

Malk, Mattias (2018). Gallery of Slavutych.

Assignment

1
First decide on a site, issue and target group you wish to engage. Design the stickers with these three factors in mind. Where will they be placed? What kind of visual language do they use? How big are they? The text must be legible, short and to the point.

2
Install the stickers in the selected locations, observe and record reactions.

3
Depending on your message and aim, it might be useful to ask for immediate responses or conduct some interviews after the stickers have been up for some time. Did people notice them? Did they understand the message? Do they agree or disagree and why? How did the intervention impact their understanding of the space itself or its socio-political roots?

4
Reflect on the findings. What did you learn? What worked, what did not and why? What changed during the intervention? How has your perception of the place and its inhabitants changed? For longer projects you might want to consider if the intervention had any lasting impact.

5
Decide if the experiment needs to be repeated. If not, then draw your conclusions and finalise the research.

assignment

Making Material Sense

An aspiration for the poetry of matter

Willie Vogel
Studio Inscape / Faculty of Architecture, Delft University of Technology

The materiality of our built environment provides the surface on which to write or tell a tale and thus form traces of unfulfilled desires or entries for reflection. Yet, materials are silent, stay often unnoticed and are taken for granted. In a world where much attention is given to the immaterial and virtual interactions, this exercise focuses specifically on the *manifestation* of these interactions. The goal of this exercise would be to unfold the material assemblages of our environment and trace its ethics through aesthetics. In other words, the physical appearance of a building will be observed and investigated in greater detail to understand why certain materials come together at that specific site. This way, things like geology, climate, craft, politics, and societal development will surface in our material culture.

The materials of facades, porches, pavements, or roofs are decisions taken by architects or craftsmen working in larger social systems. Locally sourced or imported from far away, site specific or conforming to global standards, cheap or of great expense; the choice and usage of material is a serious and critical one. Bearing this in mind, it is important to emphasise that materials always come from somewhere, are formed by someone and are used by another, our usage and moulding of materials is a sentient act.

To do justice to the multiple ecologies composing our built environment this exercise aims to lay bare both scientific and poetical readings. By combining the poet's free eye of imagination with more scientific knowledge, our built environment will appear more approachable. The science fiction writer, Le Guin (2017, p. 16), states that poetry is a language that speaks "for" the thing through its qualitative relationship with the individual human or depicting the thing itself – from the inside. The material itself is not anymore reducible to an inert substance composed of physicochemical processes (Coole and Frost 2010, p. 9). Furthermore, a poetic description allows us to look at the relational aspects of that specific material. In our merely human composed environments, the material used to build will merge with the other (in)organic matters abutting. In the case of our towns and cities, "what is manifest arrives through humans but is not entirely because of them," (Bennett, 2010, p. 17).

In this exercise the poem will be a starting point to set focus. From here one can slowly move to larger scales. By focussing on for example the concept of a *Siedlung*, like in the poem above, one can research that the building layout was always organised as such to gain as much light, air, and sun. During that time this was the living standard, composing cheap houses made from bricks with a plaster coat (currently in need of renewal). Geological resources, craft, Zeitgeist, politics, and city identity come together in this one building around the corner cited in the poem above. In other words, by describing our built environment in a poetic and scientific way it renders our attention sideways – looking to and through our environmental ecologies. This not only helps to build an identity and deeper connection for the city-dweller but might also help in further developments of the neighbourhood.

> One or two new windows, double-glazed
> Only a view wooden shutters left
> acing curtains as bequest
> meanwhile
> the renovation narrative is phrased
> A steel structures rise
>
> Brick is visible where plaster waned
> Pale, old appeared, a previous century relic
> More than three hundred with Light, air and sun
> A Siedlung covering the block while courtyards, playfields framed
>
> The corners are triple serrated
> Topped off with a red wooden crown
> Skin of horizontal stripes of yellow plaster all the way down
> And orange, purple English Cross Bond alternated

References

Bennett, J. (2010). *Vibrant matter.* Duke University Press.

Coole, D., & Frost, S. (2010). Introducing the new materialisms. In *New materialisms: Ontology, agency, and politics*, 1-43.

Le Guin, U.K. in Tsing, A. L., Bubandt, N., Gan, E., & Swanson, H. A. (Eds.). (2017). *Arts of living on a damaged planet: Ghosts and monsters of the Anthropocene.* University of Minnesota Press.

Further reading

Jacobus, M. (2012). *Romantic Things.* University of Chicago Press.

Tsing, A.L. (2015). *The Mushroom at the End of the World.* Princeton University Press.

Assignment

1
Walk around the neighbourhood and pick a specific building.

2
Observe and scrutinise the building's materials, the details, the inhabitants, the plants attached, and its relationship with the street. Write a few lines of your observation as a poem.

3
Review the poem you made and see which parts beg for extra investigation.
Questions you could ask yourself include:
- From which building period does this building date, and what were the material standards? Where are the local material sources?
  In which development state was the city when the building was erected?

4
Rewrite and add the additional information in the poem. This rewriting part adds the scientifical layer without losing the poetic one. This way round helps to reduce the scientific information to the most pivotal.

5
Reflect on the poem. The following questions may help:
- Change the materials mentioned in the poem to reflect on the importance of each material. Does a substitution leave the building unchanged, or will a new building arise?
- Read the poem to someone else and see if the building is recognisable? Does the recipient miss elements or materials?

6
Hopefully the focus on materiality gives not only a better reading of the environment but also a vision or appreciation to specific local materials and an ethical awareness of the building culture. This generates a sense of identity and connection for inhabitants and can help city developers and architects in their future projects.

Mapping Graffiti and Street Art
The construction of meaningful itineraries

method

Clara Sarmento
Centro de Estudos Interculturais, ISCAP, Politécnico do Porto

Often confused, graffiti and street art are both movements of contemporary art viewed as subversive, displayed in public spaces and closely related. In general, graffiti exhibits the name and the territory of the author, it is a codified message for other graffiters, indifferent to public recognition. Street art is informative, polysemic and/or multimodal, and authors want the public to see and relate to their artworks. Graffiti communicates between restricted groups, it is an internal, secrete language, among those who are able to decipher codified signatures and appreciate writing styles. Street art communicates at a conceptual and open level with the public in general, using humour, irony, aesthetics, and the absurd.

Graffiti and street art function as unexpected sensorial stimuli and uncensored intellectual challenges during the everyday experience of the city. We propose a method for mapping digital routes of graffiti and street art, that express site-specific dynamics and reflect urban cultural geographies, in the open, unstable space of the city. By mapping these routes, meaningful itineraries emerge and walking becomes an immersive experience, instead of a mechanical displacement of the body.

The democratic use of the urban space also entails a free, personal interpretation of the artworks inscribed on the walls. Map builders are asked to pick their way through the conglomeration of images, symbols, colours, letters, materials and types that pervade the pages of the streets, in order to read the book that is the city. Thus, instead of portaying the city as a labyrinth, mapping generates a self-conscious positioning as well as a living understanding of the urban fabric.

What might seem threatening and disconcertingly unclassifiable to some passersby, can be protective and aesthetically inspiring for others. Graffiti and street artworks combine the exhilaration that the city offers and the isolation that creation demands. Street artists build their own networks of connection, movement, and meaning. However,

Route of S. Bento, Porto: POI "Rua da Madeira". This image image belongs to the project StreetArtCEI, developed by the Center for Intercultural Studies of the Polytechnic of Porto. Credits: Clara Sarmento and StreetArtCEI project.

artworks and painting sites are linked by street, bus or underground rail maps. Therefore, through a sequence of: a) observant walking through the streets, b) photographing artworks, c) localising artworks on a map, and, d) tracing the routes that connect them, the unspoken networks of graffiti and street art emerge. This method intends to map the spatial patterns of urban creativity, starting from the actual experience of moving through the cultural territory of the city.

Graffiti and street art are produced to be discovered and decodified, instead of passively consumed. As such, they deconstruct the traditional role of studios, galleries and museums, where art is confined within delimited, surveilled spaces. Graffiti and street art works are accessible to everybody and become part of the city's routine. The material dimension of the city is related to the physical production of graffiti and street art, which establishes a dialogue with the edified environment. Works are composed not only of graphic contents, but also of the physical characteristics and textures of their supports. Even time itself is part of the dimension artists confer to their ephemeral works. Meaning is found in the processes of social construction, therefore, there are to two possible layers of meaning in graffiti and street art works: the internal narrative (the story told) and the external narrative, i.e. the social context that produces the image and sustains the framework of its interpretation, when visualised.

References

StreetArtCEI is an open archive of digital routes of graffiti and street art in Porto and other medium-sized cities of Northern Portugal. StreetArtCEI mapped more than 4500 images collected between 2017 and 2022, distributed along 14 routes, organised in 33 maps and 372 Points of Interest (POIs).

Futher readings

Campos, R., & Sarmento, C., eds. (2014) *Popular and Visual Culture. Design, Circulation and Consumption*. Newcastle upon Tyne: Cambridge Scholars Publishing.

Collier, M. (2001). Approaches to analysis in visual anthropology. In Theo Van Leeuwen & Carrey Jewitt (Eds.). *Handbook of Visual Analysis* (35-60). London: Sage Publications.

Sarmento, C. (2020). Methodological Proposals and Critical Responses for the Study of Graffiti and Street Art: The project StreetArtCEI. SAUC – *Street Art & Urban Creativity Scientific Journal*, 6(2), 24-47.

Silva, L. (2018). *Filling the gap: Um projeto social de graffiti e street art no Grande Porto*. Dissertation in Intercultural Studes for Business. Porto: ISCAP-P:PORTO.

Silva, L. (2019). Graffiti e street art: Manifestações estéticas no Grande Porto. *Revista Sensos-E*, 6(3), 124-37.

Assignment

1
Drift at random through the city, feel the city, observe the walls.

2
Photograph graffiti and street artworks, including both illegal and commissioned -pieces, whether they stand in high-visibility tourist spots, or in remote alleys of the outskirts.

3
Take notes; record the location of graffiti and street art works, as well as emerging sensations, thoughts, impressions, and interrogations.

4
Pinpoint the location of photographed graffiti and street artworks on a free digital collaborative map (e.g. Google My Maps). Each location becomes a Point of Interest (POI), designated by the name of the respective street, alley, square, park, building, etc.

5
A POI might include any number of graffiti and street artworks, from one to infinite.

6
Upload the photos of the graffiti and street art works of each POI to the map. Feel free to add comments.

7
Link the several POI and observe the itinerary designed on the map.

8
Compare the itinerary with existing street, bus or underground rail maps.

9
Generate a route that can be travelled along under normal conditions, starting and/or ending near an accesible landmark. Provide a name to each route created.

10
Walk, experiment and correct the route, if needed. Occasionally return to the route and update the map with new POI and photos of graffiti and street art works created in the meantime.

assignment

Meaning-making

Urban semiotic analysis

method

Mattia Thibault
Language Unit, Tampere University

Semiotics, as a discipline and a field of studies, focuses on "semiosis," that is the creation and circulation of meaning. It does so by investigating signs, texts, languages and their relations and hierarchies within cultures. Many semioticians have turned their attention to the anthropic environment that is the richest in semiotic potential: the city. Urban semiotics investigates how urban spaces create, mediate, and circulate meaning and, according to the focus of the analysis, the method can be applied to a specific space (a plaza, a neighbourhood), a single element (a monument) or an entire city.
If we look at the city as a semiotic space, we can understand it as a dynamic element that can be read, at any given moment, as a text (Barthes, 1967). A city, however, is a peculiar text: it is extremely choral, as it has countless authors across history, and it is continuously written and re-written. A semiotic analysis of the city brings different dynamics to the surface and compares them. The analysis will proceed by layers, starting from what is there and then progressively trying to reconstruct the dialogues, hierarchies and symbols of the urban spaces. These layers are:

1. **Texts and contexts**. The elements of the city (buildings, monuments, plazas, fountains) are meaningful on their own, but they acquire meaning also from the urban context around them, they are immersed in a constant dialogue with the elements that surround them as well as with the city itself. Some specific elements, especially monumental ones, can also shine an aura of context all around them, influencing whole neighbourhoods or entire cities.
2. **Borders, centres and peripheries**. The city embodies and crystallises the shape of its symbolic universe, or 'semiosphere' (Lotman, 1990). The organisation of the spaces of the city reflects the sociocultural dynamics of its inhabitants. Urban borders, centres and peripheries reflect ideological hierarchies. The cathedral in the centre of a medieval city, and the bank-owned skyscraper towering over a contemporary city both reflect the centrality of, respectively, religion and capitalism over the cultures of each city.
3. **Historical strata**. Some of the elements of the city can resist through centuries (such as the city's orientation grid), while others

A picture of the *Fearless Girl* sculpture by Kristen Visbal, and the *Charging Bull* by Arturo Di Modica in Wall Street, New York. The relation between the two statues and their location, as well as the authorial dynamics behind it (Di Modica first placed its sculpture abusively, while the *Fearless Girl* was placed later, as part of an advertising campaign) all showcase some of the relevant semiotic dimensions of cities. Photo: ©Antony Quintano, Creative Commons.

change swiftly (like advertising boards). These elements coexist, the older determining the new ones, the new ones overwriting the old ones.

4 **Conflicts**. Conflicts that take place are recorded in the urban writings in the form of petrified struggles for prominence, centrality, and traffic between religious, political and economic powers, as well as bottom up attempts to reclaim the right to write the city (as in DIY urbanism and street art).

5 **Enunciations**. An urban text can be written and can be read, but it can also be enunciated: it can be actualised and brought to life by the practices that take place in it. These practices, lifestyles, and events contribute to the meaning of the city.

6 **Symbolism and representations**. Representations of cities can strongly influence their meanings and perception. From Frank Sinatra's New York, New York to Dumas' Three Musketeers, these representational elements, while not physically present in the city, are embedded in the ways their inhabitants and visitors understand – and love – them.

A semiotic analysis can focus deeply on one of these layers, reconstructing and mapping the meaning of the spaces analysed, or compare and contrast several ones, looking for the synergies and contradictions between different levels.

Meaning-making

References
Barthes, R. (1967). Sémiologie et urbanisme, in Barthes, *L'aventure sémiologique*, Seuil, Paris.

Lotman J. M. (1990). *Universe of the Mind, a Semiotic Theory of Culture*, I.B. Tauris & Co, London.

Further readings
Bellentani F., Panico, M. and L. Yoka (2023). *Research Agendas in Urban Semiotics*. Edward Elgar Publishing.

Examples / Applications
Lagopoulos, A.P. (2005). Monumental urban space and national identity: the early twentieth century new plan of Thessaloniki. *Journal of Historical Geography*, 31(1), 61-77.

Thibault, M. (2021). San Francisco, Japan: Urban Cultural Hybridizations in Big Hero 6 and The Man in the High Castle. In *Western Japaneseness: Intercultural Translations of Japan in Western Media*, Vernon Press, 71-88.

Assignment

1
Familiarise yourself with the urban space that you want to analyse: walk the spaces, get acquainted the history and culture, look at the most topical representations.

2
Select a specific area of the city (a neighbourhood, a street, a plaza) in order to circumscribe your analysis. You can use a map of the area as well as taking pictures to support your analysis.

3
Look at the layer of *texts and contexts*. What urban elements are present and significant? How do they influence each other's meanings? What kind of dialogue emerges from their relations, both semantic and spatial? Try to make them on the map and take pictures of them. Reconstruct schematically their relations.

4
Try to distinguish between the different historical *strata* of the city. What has been maintained through time? Have these urban elements preserved their original functions, or have they been assigned new meanings? What are the latest additions? What is their relationship with older ones?

5
Reconstruct the *petrified conflicts*. What socio-political struggles and dynamics emerge from the urban morphology and architecture?

Which actors (organisations, individuals, companies) have been able to write the city and represent themselves in it? Who seems to be missing (i.e. who did *not* have the possibility to influence the city)?

6
Compare the different layers. Is it possible to reconstruct when the petrified conflicts took place? Were they synchronic (different powers writing the city at the same time) or diachronic (someone tried to erase or overwhelm an earlier writing at a later time)? What is the role of the single texts within these conflicts? How are contexts used in this specific location?

7
Investigate the *synergies and contradictions* among these different layers. How do different elements converge to say the same story (and whose story is that)? How do other elements propose different perspectives and positions (e.g. a graffiti defacing a monument)?

8
Finally, try to reconstruct the overall meaning-making dynamics of the chosen location. What does the space communicate holistically? How do all the different elements and layers analysed participate in the overall sense of the place?

(multi)Styling Places ...with Queneau

method

Esteban Restrepo Restrepo
École Nationale Supérieure d'Architecture de Paris-La Villette

When dealing with urban places (conceived or not by architects) represented by the literary medium (writing), we often tend to observe *what* is represented, rather than *how* it is represented. That means that we usually limit our understanding of these urban places to their very diegetic characteristics, and leave aside the artistic medium – the literary language – in which they are expressed. This restrictive approach is explicitly condemned by French philosopher, Louis Marin (1994, p.255), who argues that, "the whole historical imagery of description and mimesis is built on the transitive dimension of representation (that is, representing something) by forgetting its reflective opacity and its modalities (that is, presenting something)."[1]

In 1947 French writer, Raymond Queneau, wrote *Exercices de Style*, one among many of his experimental works, in which he followed the precepts of the group known as OULIPO he founded with the mathematician, Francois Le Lionnais. OULIPO is an acronym for *Ouvroir de Littérature Potentielle*, that we could roughly translate as 'Workshop of Potential Literature'. In this singular text, Queneau imposes to himself a strict and precise constraint consisting of telling an anodyne urban event in 99 ways, each one of them in a different style. The event in question refers to a person who witnesses an altercation between an eccentrically dressed man and another passenger within a bus in Paris, and then sees the same man two hours later at the St-Lazare Train Station getting advice on adding a button to his overcoat. Among these 99 retellings, we can find styles such as: Dreamy style, Metaphoric style, Retrograde style, Hesitative style, Official Letter style, Onomatopoetic style, Philosophic style, Sonnet style, Olfactory style, Tactile style, Ode style, Medical style, Zoological style, Probabilistic style, Portrait style, etc.

The multiplication of a single urban fact in 99 different ways of telling it, in which each version focuses on a special tonality and the explicit intention that comes with, unsettle the reader for a moment who inevitably sees how the unequivocal nature of the fact itself tends to be dissolved. In Queneau's work, what finally matters is the expression, which is never neutral or objective; the aesthetical treatment of language involves a lot of artistic decisions, such as the choice by the author of a point of view from which the narrator will relate the story, the choices regarding the verb-tenses, the ones related to the connotative and denotative characteristics of each lexical particle, and to the syntax that implies a rhythm and an intonation. All these, among many language possibilities, are going to have a direct incidence on the very perception of the fact/event.

Queneau´s Exercices de Style seem to take into account Louis Marin´s historical criticism of description and mimesis in regard to a phenomenology of representation, to produce what we might call a hypertext: the cohabitation of multiple representations of a single fact in order to deconstruct it, and where the qualities of expression – the how – get the upper hand of the objective fact – the what.

Now, Exercices de Style is not, strictly speaking, a scientific method because there is not any demonstrative intention in Queneau´s work. What we can see here is rather a creative tool or a literary device conceived and developed by the writer to exhaust the linguistic possibilities of a place in order to create a kaleidoscopic vision of it.

Note

1 *"Toute la fantasmatique de la description et de la mimesis s´est édifiée sur la dimension transitive de la représentation (représenter quelque chose) par oubli de son opacité réflexive et de ses modalités (se présenter)."* Marin, L. (1994). *Mimésis et description. In De la Représentation*, Paris: Seuil/Gallimard, 255.

References

Marin, L. (1994). Mimesis et description. In *De la Représentation*, Paris: Seuil/Gallimard.

Queneau, R. (1947). *Exercices de Style*. Paris: Gallimard.

Queneau, R. (1958). *Exercises in Style*, translated by Barbara Wright. London: Gaberbocchus Press.

(multi)Styling Places

Assignment

1
Look around, whether you are in a coffee shop, a park, or at the window of your apartment and focus on the actions each person you see does.

2
Wait until something happens that you find interesting, an event (it does not have to be necessarily odd).

3
Write down the description of the event focusing on the person(s) involved, the postures of their bodies, the objects they are using while the event in question occurs, and the way they use the space they are in. No corrections allowed during the writing. (That is your (first and spontaneous) style).

4
Now, re-write what you have written again, make some improvements, change whatever you need to change. (Reflect on the intentions behind these changes. What moves to make these alterations?... That would be your edited/critique de style).

5
Re-write your text again thinking of one single recipient (a 5-year-old girl, the President of France, a bird, etc.) you will address your text to. How did this new person affect your initial writing (and force you to create a new style)?

6
Think how your father and mother would tell the event in question. Write the two versions focusing on their own different characters. (Was it difficult to put yourself (and write) in other´s shoes?)

7
Now take one of these versions and erase all the adjectives. (What happened? Did you like the result? How did you find it?)

8
Take another version and remove all the commas, and rebuild the text again (without using commas) trying to keep its meaning. (Did you manage to do it? Did the operation inevitably create another sense of what you meant initially?)

9
Now is your time to play and create your own style rules. Write two new versions of the event following your formal interests.

10
Reflect on what happened to the event as you perceived and described it for the first time after re-writing it ten times in ten different styles during the real-isation of this assignment (that reflection would be, also, another exercise in style).

Performing (on) Architecture through Theatre Protocols

method

Filip Jovanovski and Ivana Vaseva
Faculty of things that can't be learned / FR~U

Marija Mano Velevska
Faculty of Architecture, University Ss. Cyril and Methodius, Skopje

This method translates theatre-making protocols into the urban context to be implemented within a particular building. Despite the static posture of buildings, the method activates space through aesthetic and ethical processes, creating relations between architecture, visual and performing arts, and film in a cross-disciplinary approach that extends the scope of each one of these arts. The main outcome is an event as an experiential and emotional artistic endeavour that advocates for new meanings in the public and collective realm.

The artistic-curatorial duo, Filip Jovanovski and Ivana Vaseva, has applied this method on several occasions on different projects and performances over the last decade, shedding light on particular buildings with historical and political relevance. They explore the influence of the neoliberal reality on post-socialist societies that endure the pervasive changes of their local socio-spatial context, and call for an urgent construction of new mechanisms and methods that citizens can appropriate in order to cope with rapid changes in their built environment and everyday life.
The method is based on an analogy with typical theatre-making protocols consisting of five steps: (1) Choosing a text/drama, (2) Dramatic reading with actors at a table, (3) Text adaptation for a specific stage and audience, (4) Rehearsals on stage with actors, and (5) The final outcome: the premiere (Идризи, 2020).

In the first two steps, a building with social, historical and architectural relevance in a given context is chosen and taken as a text to be investigated. Thus, collecting relevant information about it and consulting professionals and official institutions is crucial during these first phases; a close cooperation with local community is required as well, in order to collect personal viewpoint(s), memories, and stories.
The third and the fourth steps are fundamentally creative acts where the collected data and information are transferred into new narratives. The specific combination of facts and fiction, and narration and acting in a direct form of communication has the aim of pulling the audience into a walk-through of historical synchronicities, creating a

(left) Dear Republic – Performance essay for the Post office building in Skopje, 2021. Photo: Ljubica Angelkova. (right) Reading the Post-office building. Sketch for a performance / Workshop 'Lost and Found'. Photo: Filip Jovanovski.

building's emotional chronicle. For example, in the performance, *This building talks truly* – the biography of the Railway Residential Buildings in Skopje is narrated through the life episodes of its residents, verified and made-up – stories are interweaving: one out of three stories are fictional, such as the one about the architect, Bogdanović, staying in the building (fiction) shortly after fleeing the political regime to a neighbouring country and before reaching his final destination (true), which is quite possible since he was for sure in Skopje in that period. The premiere is the final step, and is a public on-site event; an interactive performance where actors, space and audience actively co-participate. This event found inspiration in the second point of Jean-Luc Godard's (1970) manifesto, *What is to be done?*

This performative action based on productive research and experimental artistic practices aims to establish relationships between public spaces and historical and urban narratives through the process of rediscovering meanings. Looking at historically rooted continuities/discontinuities of specific sites, this method serves as a tool for artists, architects, urban planners, politicians and historians, to rethink and reconceptualise the city as a vibrant, dynamic, and sustainable habitat, but equally aims to give citizens a proactive role in the process of creating new meanings for a place. Through its formal appearance (on-site performance), people and buildings are brought together in an interesting play of roles: the building becomes a stage, citizens become actors, architecture becomes scenography, community problems become text, and the performance itself becomes a tool for policy transformations.

Performing (on) Architecture

References
Идризи, Бесфорт (2020, IV) Ова зграда (у)истину говори: Од јавног (заједничког) простора до простора за Перформанс In: Милош Латиновић (ed.) *Сцена Часопис за позоришну* уметност Нови Сад
https://www.pozorje.org.rs/wp/wp-content/uploads/2021/02/Scena-4-2020-web2.pdf?fbclid=IwAR0LDk509akA5fWXu-oora_tAOO-j2ExBKHtTAOcpu4CAjGggBYzkRD-pctDo

Godard, J.L. (1970). The manifesto *What is to be done?*
http://www.derives.tv/Que-faire

Further readings
Jovanovski, F., Vaseval. & Lelovac, K. (2021). This Building Talks Truly. In Ana Vilenica (Ed.) *Radical Housing: Art, Struggle, Care*, Amsterdam: Institute of Network Cultures.

Lelovac, K. Jovanovski, F. (2018). Building as a stage-community problems as a text, theatre performance as a process of policy making. In *Theatre between Politics and Policies. New Challenges. International Scientific Conference.* Faculty of Drammatic arts, Belgrade, Serbia.

Vaseva, I. & Jovanovski, F. (2019). *This Building Talks Truly*. Skopje: Museum of the City of Skopje.

Examples/ Applications
Васева,И. Јовановски, Ф., (2015). *111 тези за ГТЦ* (111 Theses for GTC), Skopje: Faculty for things that are not taught.
https://okno.mk/node/42597https://okno.mk/node/46643

Golden Triga This Building Talks Truly, Republic of North Macedonia,
http://www.pq.cz/awards-winners/
https://akto-fru.org/en/1698-2/

Performance essay *Universal Hall in Flames: Tragedy in Six Decades*
https://mkc.mk/en/event/universal-hall-in-flame-27-11/

Assignment

1
Select a building (text). It needs to have a societal, historical and/or architectural and artistic relevance.

2
Define certain problems in the local context related to the selected building (drama).

3
Compile information on the building (research): its history, usage, architecture. For this step various sources are possible: archival material, newspaper clippings, architectural layouts, photographs, as well as interviews with users and/or inhabitants, personal stories and/or rumours.

4
Rewrite the stories (historical and personal) using fictional interventions in order to highlight the meanings communicated by/with/in the building.

5
Define the most suitable artistic form of expression for the new stories (singing, speaking, acting, light, music, video, written text, slogans, photography, scenography, or spatial interventions) and select the actors (it is not necessary that all the performers are professionals).

6
Rehearse on stage (site specific/urban context) with the text/script already written.

7
Define the mise-en-scène, focusing on the architectural configuration, so that every act of the performance is represented in a different space.

8
Decide on tactics of involving the audience within the performance (physical interactions or dialogues), in order to allow them take active part of it and explore the building.

9
Live performance ('premiere').

Performing the City from Cyberspace

method

Juliana Wexel and Mirian Estela Nogueira Tavares
Centro de Investigação em Artes e Comunicação, Universidade do Algarve, Faro

The rise of artistic events performed at a distance through digital interfaces highlights the possibility of a cyber-stage practice that imposes a redefinition of the various elements of performance, such as space, body, time, and audience (Bardiot, 2013). 'Cyberperformance,' also termed networked performance, telematic or digital performance (Dixon, 2007), covers artistic initiatives that involve the performing arts, such as theatre, performance, dance, music and that make use of digital and computational technologies in technical and aesthetic conceptions. Another example is the term, *cyberformance*, which was first used by Helen Varley Jamieson (2000) to identify a specific artistic genre of performances and theatre where performers/actors and audience meet synchronously in virtual space.

We propose a dynamic method applied to post-digital artistic practices involving the concept of *hybrid space*: the space of combination between physical objects and digital information-communication networks; a combination between virtual and actual space and between physical concrete space and digital ephemeral space (Tira, 2021). The objective is to suggest an experimental, unorthodox, disruptive, and generative methodological resource for creative processes based on digital media art. This method would in turn make it possible to produce and reveal new narratives, as well as imaginative, visually aesthetic dimensions using the urban space as a character, object or stage to the artistic interventions. The method is indicated for the development of projects and artefacts of artistic intervention that mediate urban spaces and digital spaces. We have dubbed this method: *CyberPerformanCity*, a portmanteau word elaborated from the lexical *cyberperfomance* (Dixon, 2007) and city, allied to the quality of *cyberperformativity* (Varley Jamieson, 2000). CyberPerformanCity is based on three premises: a) Performance art as a strategy of artistic expression; b) The use of Digital Tools/Online platforms/Cyberspace in the creation process and/or mediation with the audience; c) The use of urban space as a subject, object or platform for artistic work. The method is directed towards: a) Artists interested in the development of artistic artefacts in the context of urban media art, considering that, "a still emerging and rapidly developing domain in public art, constantly transforming and forging new relationships with technology,

On the left, visual artist, Rafa Monteiro (@RafaMon, on Instagram) poses in panorama next to the graffiti "Yara" (2018), created on a gable in the cove of Botafogo, Rio de Janeiro, Brazil, in one of the most famous tourist destinations in the world, with Sugarloaf Mountain in the background. On the right, Albanian architect Dorina Pllumbi shares via Instagram her experience (Selfiecity) with the work trans-mediated into a digital filter "Yara" via Spark AR Studio.
Source: *Make me up!*

architecture, design, science, biology, urban development, film, music, performance, and other disciplines, has been privileged." (Toft, 2016, p. 52); b) artists and artist-activists interested in developing works with disruptive characteristics, whether in language, aesthetics or thematic fields (feminist, queer, post-colonial, ecological, racial, social) that use the urban space as a stage and work platform; c) artists-researchers who are inspired by new methodologies for the development of digital artistic projects inspired by urban space. Based on practice-based research (Candy, 2006), *CyberPerformanCity's* methodology is open, generative, modular and adaptable to various contexts of experimental creation and research: it embraces the diversity of artistic genres, activist and disruptive actions, physical spaces and technological tools.

References

Candy, L. (2006). Practice-Based Research: A guide. *CCS report*, 1(2). University of Technology, Sydney.

Dixon, S. (2007). *Digital Performance: A History of New Media, Performance Art, and Installation.* The MIT Press.

Jamieson, H. V. (2008). *Adventures in cyberformance* (Doctoral dissertation, Queensland University of Technology).

Manovich, L. (2017). *Instagram & Contemporary Image.* Postdigital Aesthetics.

Papagiannouli, C. (2011). Cyberformance and the Cyberstage. *The International Journal of the Arts in Society*, 6(4). 273-282.

Scolari, C. (2013). *Narrativas transmedia: cuando todos los medios cuentan.* Deusto.

Tira, Y. (2021). *Digital Urban Art in Historic City Centers in Times of Democratic.* InTransforming Urban Nightlife and the Development of Smart Public Spaces Transition. Istanbul Technical University.

Toft, T. (2016). *What urban media art can do. In What Urban Media Can Do: Why, When, Where & How.* ISBN 978-3-89986-255-3. Deutschland: Avedition. 50-65.

Wexel, J. (2021). Theater, Audiovisual and Streaming: an Analysis of Theater-Making in Times of Pandemic Uncertainty in the Post-Dramatic Experience of the Play Waiting for Godette. *Rotura - Revista de Comunicação, Cultura e Artes*, (1), 39-46.

Example/Application

Wexel, J., Pereira, S. (2021). Make me up!: Uma proposta de artefacto digital performativo em tempos de ressignificação da arte urbana pós-pandemia. in: *Proceedings of ARTECH 2021: 10th International Conference on Digital and Interactive Arts. Hybrid Praxis-Art, Sustainability.* Aveiro, Portugal. October 13 - 15, 2021. ACM Association for Computing Machinery.

Wexel, J. (ed.) (2021). Video Performance *Make me up!* https://www.instagram.com/tv/CVAOiyPKRqE/?utm_medium=copy_link

Acknowledgement

The CyberperformanCity method is circumscribed in the CyPET Project (FCT-UAlg-ISMAI-Portugal)

Assignment

The following assignment is inspired by the creation process of the artefact Make me up! via Spark AR Studio, which used a facial recognition-based virtual filter with Augmented Reality technology to create cyber-performative narratives between street art made by feminist artists and social media. (You can find out more about it on Instagram: @makemeup.artproject). You can download the Spark AR Studio application for free on sparkar.facebook.com.

1
Choose and photograph a piece of street art that is part of your everyday life.

2
Identify what kind of topic might be expressed or implied in the artistic intervention and reflect on the work's artist-activist discourse.

3
Use a digital tool, such as Spark AR Studio or Photoshop, to model the image so that it is adaptable to the idea of a mask.

4
After modelling the mask, make tests of the mask prototype with known people, taking into account the diversity of faces (shapes, gender, age, ethnicity, etc.).

5
Perform with the image in public space, in the form of a selfie (Selfiecity, Manovich, 2017) or connect it with some new element such as surrounding objects, other faces, columns, walls, streetlights, or spaces that already have an urban artistic intervention in order to amplify the discourse identified in the interaction with the original work.

6
Submit the images for public use on social media such as Instagram and Facebook. If you know the authorship and title of the street artwork, use them as the title of the filter to enhance the dissemination of the original work. Otherwise, name the filter with the place's name where the work was found or choose a title based on the work's discourse.

7
Observe the feedback from the sharing of work on social networks, according to step 6. Talk to the public about their experience if they also used the filter(s) and reflect on the results of the experience.

8
Reflect on the outcome of the whole experience: what meanings and/or narratives did the performative interaction produce in the public space?

Planning and Walking Thematic Routes

Emilio J. Gallardo-Saborido, Escuela de Estudios Hispano-Americanos / Instituto de Historia (IH), CSIC, Sevilla

Francisco J. Escobar Borrego, Faculty of Philology, Universidad de Sevilla

Thematic routes constitute an attractive resource for scientific dissemination. They give us a chance to explore cities while walking, chatting and sharing knowledge on urban cultural heritage, with the guidance of experts and following a predesigned route and a coherent audio-visual narrative. Then, contents related to history, urban design, art, paintwork, music or literature, for instance, can be adapted in order to present them in a didactic and entertaining way to a wide variety of audiences.

In addition, digital resources make it possible to create suggestive hybrid experiences in which the participants of these routes can interact with tangible and intangible heritage. In this way, digital resources improve the essential meaning that heritage arouses and awakens in local communities. Digital resources often even favour the appropriation of heritage because they provide local communities with specific and concrete ways to project their feelings, emotions, and, in short, their sensitive and sensory senses on their own environments.

Diving deeper into the different stops that make up the route will result in progressively discovering aspects and details that were at first not recognisable and, on occasion, even somewhat secret because they are superimposed through layers, strata and edges which form an authentic cultural palimpsest of a reticular and polyhedral nature. Besides the monuments, plaques, or inscriptions and poems transferred to stone that pay homage to and recall outstanding figures, characters, or historical-literary events; the houses that appeared to be neutral and devoid of meaning, in fact reveal a rich cultural memory for those attending these walks.

To design and implement a thematic route, firstly we must identify the topic we want to address. This theme is developed by making several stops that allow us to offer a coherent vision of the route from a narrative point of view. It is important to calculate the distance and the duration of the complete itinerary. The route should be adapted to a specific kind of audience and to the type of scientific dissemination activity that we are preparing (are we targeting adults, young people, children? What is their level of familiarity with the topic of the itinerary? How many participants would be an ideal number? Are there any external conditions that determine the design and implementation of the route?). Furthermore, it is advisable to design support materials for both the guides and the audience. This material can include maps and scripts with different information about each of the stops. The instructors will count with an extended version of the script where they can include all the necessary guidelines. Within this support material, you can design different kinds of assessment instruments to evaluate the impact of the activity on the participants, your performance, or the route itself.

From a didactic point of view, it is interesting to make use of multiple resources at the stops: from master speeches to group discussions or gamifications. Next, we prepare any additional material resources that may be needed, taking into account the real conditions of implementation of the itinerary (will we need microphones, tablets, smartphones?). Then, we test the result without participants in order to be aware of the external circumstances that can affect its development (light, noise, different types of spatial constraints, etc.). Once we have designed the route and verified its feasibility, we announce it through the most appropriate means and we share the script and the map with confirmed attendees. At the meeting point, we receive the participants. If we have not met the attendees previously, it is convenient to carry out some element (badge, sticker, T-shirt) that identifies us as guides. After the implementation, we deliver and check the results of the assessment instruments in order to improve a future version of the activity.

References

Escobar Borrego, F.J., & Gallardo-Saborido, E.J. (2020). Paseo científico-divulgativo a la luz de Sevilla flamenca: palimpsesto cultural. *Hispanorama. Deutscher Spanischlehrerverband*, 169(3), 32-37.

Escudero, X. & Pouzet Michel, I. (Eds.), *Le flamenco dans tous ses états*: de la scène à la page, du pas à l'image, 383-404. Shaker Verlag. http://hdl.handle.net/10261/239743

Escobar Borrego, F.J., & Gallardo-Saborido, E.J. (2021). Flamenco y divulgación científica: experiencia didáctica de la ruta Sevilla, ciudad flamenca (con pervivencia de M. Machado, Turina y *La Corte de Faraón*). In Demeyer, X. Escudero and I.P. Michel (dir.). (2021). *Le flamenco dans tous ses états: de la scène à la page, du pas à l'image.* Shaker Verlag, 383-404.

Assignment

1

Select the specific topic of your route.

2

Choose the concrete stops that you will visit considering the following tips:
a Their relevance and meaning.
b The overall distance.
c The entire duration of the itinerary.

3

Connect the stops through a coherent narrative.

4

Transfer the information to a map (you can use, for example, Google My Maps).

5

Prepare a draft and scheme containing the essential information for each stop, and make a careful selection of additional content that accompanies and complements the basic information: textual excerpts (primary and secondary sources), images, audio files, visual resources, etc.

6

Prepare a precise script of the route for those who will offer it and another one for the attendees. Remember to use accessible and pleasant language! Enrich the script with complementary resources of interest. You can add useful and attractive hyperlinks so that attendees can access to them with their electronic devices.

7

In accordance with the explanations and analysis that you will offer at each stop, it is convenient that you design didactic activities, such as educational games or topic discussions, that allow attendees to interact.

8

Prepare any electronic devices that you will need in relation to the number of attendees, and consider the environmental conditions (for instance, keep in mind the possible problems related to urban noises or the limitations of space to gather your group). Are you using a microphone, loudspeakers, tablets, etc.?

9

Disseminate the route until you have a manageable number of attendees (between 10-20 may be a suitable number). Share both the script and the route map with them.

10

Remember to identify yourself with a T-shirt or sticker prepared for the occasion. Enjoy the walk!

11

Reflect on the preparation and implementation of the route: what did you learn about your city and its micro-spaces by creating a route? Have you detected any concrete issue that might be improved in following editions?

assignment

method

Playing City-making

Negotiating natures and societies

Maarten Meijer, Charlotte von Meijenfeldt, Studio Inscape / Quintel
Eileen Stornebrink, Studio Inscape / Architecture Institute Rotterdam
(AIR) and Willie Vogel, Studio Inscape / Delft University of Technology

Recognising the (dis)connections – including possible harmonies and conflicts – between the lives of humans, plants and animals in the built environment will become all the more pertinent given the radical changes in the planet's systems, growing urban populations, and loss of biodiversity and habitat. Understanding the fluctuating and ethereal structures of (dis)connections between humans and nonhuman ecosystems is a difficult and time-consuming process (de La Bellacasa, 2017), and so we are left with little or no tools to integrate them in city-making processes.

Hence, we propose a network game as a playful and participatory tool to explore the urban 'parliament of things' by drawing on the work of Bruno Latour (2018) and other strands of post-human thought. The goal is to transform the political arena and invite more actors in city-making processes and practices. The game is a tool to improve the inclusion of human and nonhuman voices and interests, and cultivates a more eco-political sensibility in the 'players' of the game.

To set up the game, take a particular event, development plan, or problem in the urban space in question and collect information about how its different human and nonhuman inhabitant this space. When finished with this initial information gathering, use it to build a network cartography of the problem and the way in which different inhabitants relate to it as well as to each other. This network, built by the specificities and entanglements of the multiple inhabitants constructed over time, serves as the starting point for the parliament or 'game'. For the game, invite (human) stakeholders, including urban planners, architects and concerned residents, to take place in the parliamentary setting of the game, representing the wide range of concerns on the table. Using the network, the group considers consequences of particular decisions for e.g. local ecosystems, and invents and explores alternative options for negotiating between concerns and interests of all inhabitants. Using the different perspectives on the problem or event as represented in the parliament as well as the general questions provided to the players by the organisers (see step 1), players will explore and discuss different aspects of the problem in order to develop strategies of dealing with it in different ways. As such, the game will also raise a broader series of questions: whose voices and interests matter in urban development, how can more voices be included, and who has the right to decide who can stay or should leave?

References

Latour, B. (2018). Outline of a parliament of things. *Ecologie politique*, (1), 47-64.

Latour, B. and Peter Weibel, eds. (2005). *Making Things Public: Atmospheres of Democracy*. Karlsruhe: ZKM | Center for Art and Media Karlsruhe/Chicago: The MIT Press.

de La Bellacasa, M.P. (2017). Matters of care: *Speculative ethics in more than human worlds* (Vol. 41). University of Minnesota Press.

Assignment

1
Describe the problem, event or phenomenon that is the occasion for making the game. Think of one or two specific questions or problems which could be asked later to the whole group.

2
Make a list of humans and nonhuman inhabitants that are impacted positively or negatively by the problem, event, phenomenon, or possible design interventions. Go out of your way to explore the nonhuman side of things. As a rule of thumb, make sure you include:
- 3 persons (different age, ethnicity, gender)
- 3 plants (land + water)
- 3 animals (land + sky + insect)

3
Write down how each inhabitant relates to the problem, their environment, and the other inhabitants on small cards.

4
Print a map of the city or area and place the inhabitants on this map by using markers or small physical elements.

5
Each of the invited participants chooses one inhabitant. It does not matter who picks who. Every person reads their own card carefully.

6
Each participant introduces themselves and the inhabitant they represent.

7
Draw a network of dependency: lay down ropes or strings to those inhabitants you relate to. One inhabitant can have multiple connections. Without being good or wrong the network in front of you shows the interconnectedness of inhabitants on a specific site.

8
The game can begin! The development proposals can be tested as the network will show by each step what will happen to the socio-natural ecology represented in the game.

assignment

Re-Acting with Images

Respondent-generated image production and photovoice

Luc Pauwels
Faculty of Social Sciences, University of Antwerp

Respondent-Generated Image Production (RGIP) is an increasingly popular and effective visual method that comes in different forms and in different combinations with other approaches that are often grouped under the name, "visual participatory research," or, "collaborative methods" (Pauwels, 2015; Chalfen, 2020). Essentially, the RGIP method involves asking respondents to produce visual outputs (such as photographs, videos, drawings, installations etc.) in connection with a specific research question or interest. Typically, these assignments will be phrased in fairly general terms and usually relate to the immediate world and experiences of the respondent. Questions could be, for example: 'Depict the aspects of your neighbourhood that have a special meaning to you,' or, 'Make photographs of what you like and what you dislike about your present situation'. The central premise of this approach is that the resulting visual products will contain and communicate essential traits of the respondent's culture and experience, including things that are sometimes hard to put into words for various reasons. These visual products are then further analysed by the researcher, often in conjunction with the makers.

RGIP not only comprises the use of camera-based images, depicting aspects of the respondent's material world, but also includes a variety of drawing methods and techniques whereby the respondent may be prompted to give a concrete shape to more internal processes and views. "Mental mapping" is one such technique, used to bring about a person's perception of an area of interaction (e.g. which parts in a city are important or used by the respondent, or how does the respondent give sense to a place) or a complex situation. Body Mapping is another powerful technique, mainly used in health related contexts.

Whereas the purpose of RGIP in a research project is primarily to acquire unique data about the respondents' world (their visualised experiences and environment as an entry point to their culture) and thus to generate scientific knowledge, the primary aim of many

When asked by the researcher to depict crucial aspects of their life, respondents suffering from an acquired brain injury (ABI) often expressed their confusion and insecurity when trying to navigate the city through pictures depicting street signs and people reading maps. Other respondent-produced pictures referred to their need for a quiet and safe environment. (Courtesy: Alina Dragan).

photovoice and community video projects (Wang, 1999; Milne and Muir, 2020) is to initiate a positive change in the world of the participants: ideally by raising awareness of a problem in a community, empowering community members or marginalised individuals, or by trying to exert influence on authorities or policy makers to improve a problematic situation.

It is clear that RGIP researchers need to be well informed about the broader culture of the respondents to be able to adequately decode the meanings of the depicted objects and situations, as well as the way they have been visualised and organised (their 'formal' characteristics as sources of information). Researchers may most of the time see what is depicted, but they rarely know *why* exactly something is chosen by the respondents and what it means to them. So often respondent-generated images will need to be commented upon by their makers, which means that this research approach generates visual and verbal data, both of which are important to the researcher.

Asking residents or other actors involved in an urban environment to produce images is one of the most powerful ways to get into their heads: how they really experience their being in the city, how they both literally and metaphorically see the city.

References

Chalfen, R. (2020). Methodological Variation in Participant Visual Media Production. In: Pauwels, Luc and Mannay, Dawn (Eds.) *The Sage Handbook of Visual Research Methods* (2nd ed). Beverly Hills, CA/London: Sage, 239-253.

Milne, E.J. & Muir, R. (2020). Photovoice: A Critical Introduction, In: Pauwels, Luc and Mannay, Dawn (Eds.) *The Sage Handbook of Visual Research Methods* (2nd ed) 282-296.

Pauwels, L. (2015). Participatory visual research revisited: A critical-constructive assessment of epistemological, methodological and social activist tenets. *Ethnography*, 16(1), 95-117.

Wang, C. (1999). Photovoice: A participatory action research strategy applied to women's health. *Journal of Women's Health*, 8(2), 185-192.

Assignment

1
Select a group of respondents, e.g. a cross section of inhabitants of a particular neighbourhood who are willing to produce images in response to an assignment.

2
Ask them to produce 5 images showing aspects of the neighbourhood they think are problematic and 5 images of what they particularly like about their environment and its inhabitants.

3
Perform a careful analysis of what is depicted and how it is depicted. Also look for what is not depicted (i.e. negative analysis).

4
Perform a non-directive interview with the makers of the images to find out why they depicted these situations or objects and to hear their stories.

5
Compare your own analysis/interpretation of the respondent-generated images with the explanations of the respondents. To what extent do these views differ? What visible aspects were not talked about? What does this tell you about the projective, documentary, and metaphoric power of images?

6
Decide on how to present the results: a 'photovoice' exhibition/event (with an activist agenda), as a visual essay, or a scholarly article.

assignment

Re-activating Minor Matters of Archival Documents

Heidi Svenningsen Kajita
Section for Landscape Architecture and Planning,
University of Copenhagen

Can the architectural office archive, commonly ordered as a repository of building information, also reveal small social truths? Can the archive's often sparse evidence of residents' (or more generally speaking, citizens') voices be reactivated for new urban imaginaries? The archival research method put forward here in reference to the article "Urgent Minor Matters" (Kajita, 2022) gives clues about how to attend to residents' voices, and how their concerns can function in archives of mainstream design processes.

Residents, who are often not heard in planning and design processes, were invited into the site-office famously established by Ralph Erskine Arkitekter AB (REA) during the *Byker Redevelopment* in Newcastle upon Tyne, UK, between 1968 and 1983. Here, residents could speak about issues, often trivial and mundane, about their housing. Sometimes these urgent minor matters were uniquely, if sparsely, noted on paper and kept on file by the architects. To attend to these minor matters in the archive, the method adopts an analytic mode influenced by Deleuze and Guattari (2016), who wrote how the "cramped space" of "minor literature" (the literature of minorities in a majority language) amplifies connections to the wider social and political environment in which minorities operate.

In the archive, an ethnographic construction of archival research can develop knowledge and new possibilities for action (Eichhorn 2013). The archive is not seen as a storage facility but is "reactivated" by the people who use its motley records in their various ways of resistance. Documents are selected and connected in ways that bypass their usual hierarchies and roles. For example, residents' lists of complaints can lead to architects' design principles, to technical instructions, to a transcript of a radio broadcast, and to housing officers' evaluative memos. Documents are copied, transcribed, stacked and rearranged creatively in episodic orders that allow the social agency of past documents to help us imagine, reorient and even realise new worlds (Eichhorn, 2013, p. 160).

Outside the archive, a selection of documents is introduced into social and material situations. This iterative-inductive process draws on REA's own methods for taking note of residents' agency both within and beyond the office, across projects and over time. Through encounters with residents, architects and other actors, the conceptual categories are reworked to deal with how architectural communities can support residents' own activist roles in public and social housing – those whose roles are needed again, as Erskine anticipated (Erskine, 1976). Shifting positions between archival and fieldwork research, the question becomes how these historical scraps of evidence can come to function in the present and future.

The various techniques employed to attend to minor matters in the bureaucratic apparatus present us not with a unifying narrative but with possibilities for new archival and history writing. This method provides the possibility of reactivating documents and marginalia that can circulate along unordered paths, in and out of architectural design processes and storage systems, for more diverse and democratic, yet mainstream, design futures. Everything minor has a collective value. "The individual concern thus becomes all the more necessary, indispensable, magnified," claim Deleuze and Guattari (2016, p. 17), "because a whole other story is vibrating within…"

References

Deleuze, G., Guattari, F. (2016). *Kafka: Toward a Minor Literature*. Minneapolis: University of Minnesota Press.

Eichhorn, K. (2013). *The Archival Turn in Feminism: Outrage in Order*. Philadelphia, Temple University Press.

Erskine, R. (1976). Byker, *Arkitektur*, no. 8:6.

Kajita, H.S. (2022). Urgent Minor Matters – Reactivating Archival Documents for Social Housing Futures, *Architecture & Culture*. DOI:10.1080/20507828.2022.2093603

Re-activating Minor Matters

Assignment

1

"A whole other story is vibrating within …":
Select an architectural archive of interest.

2

Re-activate the architectural archive ethnographically:
Start anywhere in the archive, and trawl through as many files as you can. Often architectural archives are ordered for construction – do not follow this order when you first request and review the archival files. Know that the archive is re-activated each time it is picked up. Study documents many times over in different contexts – not only according to their architectural rationale but according to how they are used in material practices – and consider how building information embroils social agency.

3

A motley collection:
Minor matters are tangled in the dominant. They may appear in documents of all design stages, by all actors, as well as in an archive's motley collection of techniques and genres: from epic tales in documents designed specifically to inscribe residents' voices (such as a list of complaints) to the odd scribble on a technical drawing. Look for words and graphics out of place and copies that appear again and again, as if someone intervened or resisted the project's completion.

4

Activist roles are needed again:
To support those for whom 'minor matters' are urgent, and who's minor matters are dealt with in archival research, you will have to move between the archive and the field to participate in their social and material situations. Revisit the archive and field, and revise your research questions, findings and analysis continuously in support of those outside dominant power structures: those activists "whose roles are needed again."

assignment

Reading the City

Literary texts and urban writing

Onorina Botezat
Faculty of Foreign Languages and Literatures, Dimitrie Cantemir Christian University, Bucharest

Urban spaces may be read in countless ways. Within a literary text, urban narration can play different roles, from a simple description to a central part of the plot, depending on the author and genre. Urban reading may venture into the history of the city and technological developments; into the rise and fall of urban areas in neighbourhoods that define – both culturally and linguistically – a certain community; in the creation of myths and symbolisation of an urban space; or in shaping or constraining the character's behaviour. Literary images of urban spaces are fictional, mental representations based on one's own readings and as such cannot be understood other than within a certain period of time.

Henri Lefebvre (1991) interprets space as a social experience, where "architectural, urbanistic and political [...] code" (p. 4) turned into a common language shared by inhabitants of urban or rural environments, is "a code which allow[s] space not only to be 'read' but also to be constructed." (p. 7). So, if we agree to place the human being in the centre of space, he or she shall impact and craft accordingly. Thus, Lefebvre (1991, p. 73) defines the "(social) space" as something which "subsumes things produced, and encompasses their interrelationships in their coexistence and simultaneity – their (relative) order and/or (relative) disorder." And throughout history, the urban space is produced combining its reality with the imaginary discourse, labored, and narrated by its inhabitants. An urban place, be it a city or a town, is inhabited by people alike their own home, having thus a twofold impact on their lives: this space defines their identity and at the same time is proof of their own willingness to model and mould it. Both features of urban places are reflected in literature, whether plainly or within context, serving as spatial setting and identifying the character.

After finding out the answer to the main question, "Who?" and identifying the main character, the reader is eager to find clues and answers to a second question: "Where?" which reveals the space that shapes the character's identity and actions, or even becomes a character on its own terms. The description of space is a way of showing the author's intent, as well as a manner of reflecting the hero's condition and circumstances, thus establishing compositional connections between the work's parts. The role of the image of the city in literary writings grew such that it has become a character itself. The reader is absorbed in the author's reality, which is largely ensured due to categories such as artistic time and artistic space, which translate and appropriate the reality. To reveal their connection, Mikhail Bakhtin (1981), inspired by Einstein's Theory of Relativity, introduced the concept of *chronotope* as "intrinsic connectiveness of temporal and spatial relations that are artistically expressed in literature." (p. 84). Though borrowed from Kant – the idea that time and space are indispensable forms of cognition – Bakhtin uses the term to describe an immediate reality that is set to predict the literary genre, not from a "transcendental" approach.

Human space, according to Roland Barthes (1988), is the ultimate signifying space, and the city may be thought of as a type of writing. And this process may be regarded as interchangeable. The urban space may impose a style, but it also may be constructed and defined in the collective memory through imaginative discourse of different authors. Thus, urban reading may be approached from diachronic and synchronic methods of analysis. One can analyse urban space depiction in literary writings from different periods or conduct a comparative analysis of an urban space voiced by different authors from the same epoque. At the same time, this kind of incursion may be overlaid with imagological readings, asking how the city is depicted in foreign writers' literature or how it is translated, thus received, or echoed in fictional or non-fictional literature.

References

Bakhtin, M. (1981). Forms of Time and of the Chronotope in the Novel: Notes toward a Historical Poetics. In Holquist, Michael (ed.). *The Dialogic Imagination: Four Essays. Slavic Series*, no. 1. Translated by Emerson, Caryl. Austin, Texas, USA: University of Texas Press, 84–85.

Barthes, R. (1988). Semiology and Urbanism. In *The Semiotic Challenge*, translated by Richard Howard. Oxford: Basil Blackwell, 191-201.

Lefebvre, H. (1991). *The Production of Space*. Translated by Donald Nicholson-Smith. Oxford, UK: Blackwell Publishing.

Ricoeur, P. (1985). *Time and Narrative*. Volume 2. Translated by Kathleen McLaughlin and David Pellauer. Chicago: The University of Chicago.

Reading the City

Assignment

1
Choose the city that you want to focus your research on. You may have one single objective; to discover the literary image of the city diachronically, or your purpose may be twofold. After doing the first part of the research, highlighting what the common places are and how are they described in different writings from different literary époques or centuries, analyse the city's reflection in literary writings within the same generation of authors.

2
Search databases for keywords or in libraries to find several books where the action takes place in that precise city of your choice.

3
Enjoy the reading! Then find those common places, streets, squares, and neighbourhoods. Within a diachronic approach, it would be revealing to discover how the city has changed and developed. While synchronically confronted texts would emphasise different styles of writing urban places.

4
The ultimate step would be to visit the city for personal findings in terms of conclusions. As it seldom happens, we know some cities by heart from our readings.

assignment

Recapturing the City
Rhetorical analysis

method

Serap Durmus Ozturk
Department of Architecture, Karadeniz Technical University, Trabzon

'Rhetoric' indicates that the narrative has the potential of persuasion. It is not a new term and takes its roots from antiquity. However, it is constantly updated due to its potential and its meaning may evolve in different directions (Durmus, 2014). Reading and writing the city are an urban interest that aim to reveal the rhetorical relationship between narrative and architecture and its expression (Durmus Ozturk, 2021). Plural reading of urban places and creating different stories are rhetorical activities with different degrees of persuasion.

'Rhetorical analysis,' one of the narrative techniques, focuses on investigating the data of urban places and their representations, it is a literary approach examining the interactions between a text, an author, and an audience, and it narrates modes and movements in urban places. Rhetorical analysis is a form of close reading that questions how rhetorical situations are read and shaped with rhetorical principles (Rowland, 2009; Selzer, 2004). Foss (2009) explains that we use rhetorical analysis as a way of systematically investigating and classifying data and actions. Rhetorical analysis sees the research problem not as an object but as a tool for communication and it may be researched through all kinds of data concerning the city (e.g. texts, voices, sounds, interviews, routes, photographs, observations, maps, city walks, postcards, or hearing the stories of the place).

'Rhetorical modes' define the variety, the conventions, and purposes of writing narratives of urban places. It also detects and classifies the data collected for cities. The most common rhetorical modes present four genres as a representation (Lanham, 1991; Durmus Ozturk & Sadıklar, 2018): exposition, argumentation, description, and narration. Exposition includes textual content of the data, and aims to analyse data by presenting an idea and relevant evidence. Argumentation generates problems from data, and aims to present an argument to prove the validity of an idea or point of view. Unlike exposition, description aims to re-create a person, place, event or action in the data. Re-creation processes enable the real or fictional new data, because 'description' describes events that readers can later imagine. Finally, the purpose of narration is to tell a story or narrate an event(s) textually or visually. Rhetorical modes are data-related, serve to categorise data, and identify focused material for action and so on.

'Rhetorical moves' involve a series of actions to understand and make sense of the city. They are realised by smaller discourse units and analyse the use of writing the city as a narrative (Hyland, 2000; Bhatia, 2006). Rhetorical moves have three narrative prepositions used in the city/urban space and suggest what kind of activity should be done through them. The first one, 'narratives in the city,' includes the narratives that are present in the city, seeing the city as a palimpsest of multiple layers of stories. It uses activities such as writing about, listening to, looking at, walking through, drawing, mapping, reading, or observing the city. The second narrative preposition, 'narratives of the city,' includes the existing narratives (novels, poems, memoirs etc.) that depict the city. The final one, 'narratives for the city,' includes the study of alternative futures for urban places such as scenarios, and scripts. Therefore it is crucial for writers/users to ensure that they have chosen rhetorical modes and to follow rhetorical moves (narratives in/of/for the urban place).

'Rhetorical analysis' as a narrative technique looks at the connections between the urban place and the data. The collected data is classified according to the four rhetorical modes. One or more modes may be combined. Suitable actions to the chosen modes are connected through narrative prepositions: in/of/for the urban place. While rhetorical modes detect the data and its type about the city, rhetorical moves in/of/for the city identify actions of the data.

References

Bhatia, V.K. (2006). *Analyzing genre: some conceptual issues*. In M. Hewings (Ed.), *Academic writing in context: Implications and applications*. Birmingham: University of Birmingham Press. 79-92.

Durmus Ozturk, S. (2021). *Urban Narrativity. Reading, Writing and Activating Urban Places*: Methods and Assignments, Part II: Writing the City. CA18126: Writing Urban Places: New Narratives of the European City.

Durmus Ozturk, S., & Sadıklar, Z. (2018, October). *Spaces of Frida Kahlo: Rhetoric Analysis in Self-Portraits*. Journal of Near Architecture, 2(1), 56-71.

Durmus, S. (2014). *Rhetorical Construction of Architectural Thought*: Usûl-i Mi'mârî-i Osmânî (Mimarlık Düşüncesinin Retorik İnşası: Usûl-i Mi'mârî-i Osmânî). PhD Thesis. Trabzon: Karadeniz Technical University.

Foss, S.K. (2009). *Rhetorical Criticism: Exploration and Practice*. USA: Waveland Press, Inc.

Hyland, K. (2000). *Disciplinary Discourses: Social Interactions in Academic Writing*. London: Longman.

Lanham, R.A. (1991). *A Handlist of Rhetorical Terms*. London: University of California Press.

Rowland, R. (2009). *The Narrative Perspective*. In J. Kuypers (Ed.), Rhetorical Criticism. Perspectives in Action, Plymouth: MA: Lexington Books, 17-142.

Selzer, J. (2004). *Rhetorical Analysis: Understanding How Texts Persuade Readers*. In C. Bazerman, & P. M. Prior (Eds.), In *What writing does and how it does it: An introduction to analysing texts and textual practices*. NJ: Lawrence Erlbaum.

Further Readings

Riessman, C.K. (2005). *Narrative Analysis. In Narrative, Memory & Everyday Life*, Huddersfield: University of Huddersfield, 1-7.

Ryan, M.-L. (1992). *The Modes of Narrativity and Their Visual Metaphors*. Style, 26(3), 368-387.

URL-1. (2015). Retrieved from http://lakeshorehigh.stpsb.org/documents/rhetoricallistenglish3.pdf

Assignment

1
Collect one of the following kinds of data from the chosen urban place: texts, voices, sounds, interviews, routes, photographs, observations, maps, city walks, old-new postcards, hearing the stories of the place.

2
Select your rhetorical mode: exposition, argumentation, description, or narration. A combination of these is also possible.

3
Make a rhetorical move to address the urban place with narrative prepositions (narratives in/of/for the urban place).

4
Look at the connections between the collected data of the urban place and the outcomes from your chosen rhetorical mode(s) of analysis.

5
Are there indications of rhetorical effects in the connections between moves and modes in the urban place? Can the urban place convince us of what has happened or what we expect to happen? Discuss what problems have been solved by rhetorical analysis.

6
Record the rhetorical analysis as a narrative with different representations. Observe what is common and what is unique.

Revisiting Postcards

Retrospective repeat photography

method

Luc Pauwels
Department of Communication Studies, University of Antwerp

Significant changes in the appearance of cities can transpire in just a few minutes, hours or days, or span several years or even decades. 'Repeat photography' involves a diachronic study of an urban environment that focuses on changes in the urban environment that cover larger periods of time for researching social change and cultural expressions as they develop gradually in a particular physical or cultural space. Re-photography projects may start from pictures made by the researcher ('prospective studies') or depart from existing pictures ('retrospective studies', see Figures) which are often produced outside of a research context (drawn from archives, magazines, family albums, or picture post cards) (Rieger, 2020).

Repeat photography may involve re-photographing sites (e.g. exteriors and interiors: streets, gardens, homes, factories, residential areas), re-photographing *events, activities and processes* (changes in rituals, work processes or activities of a varied nature), as well as re-photographing *people* (their changing physical appearances, belongings and doings). Thus re-photography projects are not limited to revisiting environments from the same vantage point (Klett, 2020) but they may, for example, also include the visual documentation of fairs and events in the city, whether or not they take place at the same venue.

Re-photographers must realise that they are working with highly 'mediated' aspects of a presumed social reality and that, to some extent, they are revisiting views which are tied to initial choices made in the past (e.g. picture post cards of tourist attractions from a particular vantage point). Many aspects and sites of cities remain invisible in existing collections.

Another challenge for re-photography as a long term endeavour is that research subjects may disappear or become inaccessible or invisible. Structures may become broken down or hidden from view by a newly erected structure. Events may cease to exist. Participants

(Left) Antwerp Southern Docks (undated, first half of 20th century).
(Right) Southern Docks (April 2014, photo: L. Pauwels). Documenting urban change through re-photography. The Southern Docks in Antwerp were completed in 1881 for inland waterway navigation. From a thriving industrial and commercial area focused on expediting goods (mainly coal, stones, sand and mussels), which required harsh and dangerous labour by men, women and children, this neighbourhood developed into a period of destitution and neglect after the closing down of the harbour activities (1970s and 1980s), and subsequently to its present status of a highly gentrified neighbourhood with museums, art galleries, luxury lofts, restaurants and cafés. The large hydraulic power plant, 'Zuiderpershuis,' in the middle of the photographs now serves as a cultural centre, and the lower building left of the power plant, which used to be the docks' First Aid post, has become an atelier for creative writing. Currently this space is being redesigned.

may die, move away or refuse to cooperate any further. Sites may have shifted from public to private ownership, or vantage points may be inaccessible because of newly built structures, or trees that have grown bigger, and so on.

As a method, repeat photography offers a unique opportunity to study changes in cities as part of larger societies: the material culture of cities (buildings, streets, shops, open spaces etc.) as well as the observable behaviours of their inhabitants (activities, clothing, etc.) can be read as expressions of particular norms, values and expectations at a certain point in time, and camera images allow to scrutinize and document them diachronically. (Pauwels, 2020).

References

Pauwels, L. (2015). *Reframing Visual Social Science: Towards a More Visual Sociology and Anthropology*. Cambridge University Press.

Rieger, J. (2020). Rephotography for Documenting Social Change. In Luc Pauwels and Dawn Mannay (Eds.), *The Sage Handbook of Visual Research Methods* (2nd ed), 99-113.

Klett, M. (2020). Rephotography in Landscape Research. In Luc Pauwels and Dawn Mannay (Eds.) (2020). *The Sage Handbook of Visual Research Methods* (2nd ed), 114-128.

Revisiting Postcards

Assignment

1
Collect a few older postcards or historic photographs of a city you are visiting.

2
Locate the exact locations in the city from which these photographs were taken.

3
Make photographs from the same position, mimicking as much as possible the framing and perspective of the original postcard.

4
Carefully compare the two sets of photographs: what has changed in the material environment, the way people use the space, the way they look? How does this reflect social and cultural change, shifting ways of thinking with respect to the city and city life?

5
Extra option. Use these sets of images to interview locals about their city: how do they perceive these visible changes? What thoughts and reactions do these images trigger with them (making use of photo elicitation)?

assignment

Scaling Stories

Social and spatial layers of urban exploration

method

Klaske Havik
Faculty of Architecture and the Built Environment, Delft University of Technology

Scaling stories of social space' can be seen as a compact field work exercise investigating the social and spatial layers of an urban neighbourhood. In small groups, participants study public and social spaces in the area, exploring the relation between social and spatial scales. The method addresses spatial practice as dynamic interplay between urban reality, daily routines, and perceived and lived space (Lefebvre 1991, 38-39). As De Certeau suggested, these spatial practices have a narrative dimension: they are stories about people's trajectories and activities in space, and it is through stories that spatial practices can be understood (De Certeau, 1988, 115). The method 'scaling stories' explores urban places by means of storytelling, and operates on three scales: 1:1000, 1:100, and 1:10 (or 1:500, 1:50. 1:5, depending on the study area). These scales are addressed not only in spatial terms, but also in social terms; each scale refers to a person that has a relation with the site on the particular scale, i.e. has a reach in the area of that particular amount of people.

Within the framework of the social scales, the smallest scale focuses on the individual and their surroundings; the medium scale looks at communities, groups, and other forms of human organisations; and the largest scale is focused on larger populations such as those of nations or even the global scale. Aside from looking at people (or other beings), the social scales examine formal and informal groups (political, religious, administrative, working, etc.), collective and societal systems (educational, political, etc.), as well as societies and societal structures in general. Each social scale has its spatial counterpart which embodies the environment in which the social forms take place. Therefore, the smallest scale focuses on immediate surroundings of the individual such as the house or the apartment; the medium scale investigates more complex forms of architecture encompassing not only housing but also various types of public buildings and spaces intended for human interaction; and lastly, the largest scale investigates the city or other larger spatial forms.

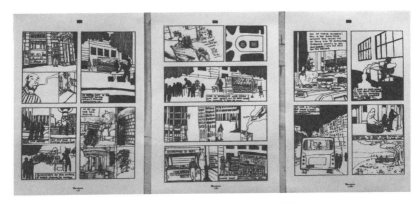

Triptych, one of the results of a workshop held in Skopje, 2019.

For each of the scales, participants first identify a local protagonist. Through an interview or a walk with the person through the neighbourhood, the participants gain insights about which places and objects are meaningful on that social and spatial scale. For each scale, the findings are documented by means of a map, a series of photographs, and a text. In the next stage, when the material of the three scales is collected, a triptych is made in which the three scales are represented side by side. In this phase, a way of representation is chosen that fits the three parallel stories. This can be a combination of map, text, photographic essay, or graphic novel.

This method was inspired by a joint workshop in London with Steve McAdam (Fluid Architecture) in 2006, with students from TU Delft and London Metropolitan university, for a site specific analysis of the Portobello road area in London. I later used the method in a workshop in Skopje with Marija Mano, Slobodan Velevski and Jana Čulek, and in a workshop at Tec de Monterrey, Guadalajara, Mexico, in 2020. While I used it mainly as a format for educational workshops on urban analysis, Jana Čulek further developed the social-spatial scale concept as a tool for comparative analysis of literary and architectural projects (Čulek 2020).

References

Čulek, J. (2020). '*Forms of Utopia. The Social and Spatial Forms of 'We' and 'Metropolisarchitecture*'. In Havik, K, Heynickx, R and Sioli, A. (Eds.) (2020). Writingplace #4 *Choices and Strategies of Spatial Imagination*. Rotterdam: nai010publishers.

De Certeau, M. (1988). *The Practice of Everyday Life*, Berkeley: University of California Press.

Lefebvre, H. (1991 [1974]). *The production of space*, London: Blackwell Publishing, London.

Scaling Stories

Assignment

1
Identify protagonists on each scale. On the scale of 1:10, you can think of a resident of a street, who would be acquainted with around ten neighbours. 1:100 could be a shop owner who sees multiple residents of the neighbourhood each day, a schoolteacher, who has a broader reach and knows the class of schoolchildren and to some extent the parents, or a member of a neighbourhood association. On the 1:1000 scale, a journalist or politician may be chosen as representative. For each of these persons, their view on the neighbourhood is different, and different spatial characteristics or objects may stand out in their view of the neighbourhood.

2
By talking with the protagonists, or by walking with them through the study area, map the daily trajectory of the character, and identify important places or objects. Make photographs, notes and sketches. Draw the map in words, identifying rhythms and encounters.

3
Write a text from the perspective of each character, describing the neighbourhood from their point of view, identifying important objects and spaces, and the way they are used in everyday life.

4
For each scale, bring the findings together. For instance by overlaying photos, maps, and text, or by making a graphic novel page presenting the daily trajectory of the characters.

5
Present the findings as a triptych of three panels, representing the study area in three scales.

assignment

method

Site-Writing

A critical spatial practice

Jane Rendell
Bartlett School of Architecture, University College London

Developing a practice of site-writing allows writing's relation to architectural and urban design to be propositional as well as analytic, experimental and open-ended while retaining precision and rigour. There are multiple ways in which this can happen: First, through an exploration of the materiality of visuospatial processes which combine written texts and images. Second, in the development of the particular spatial and architectural qualities of storytelling and narration. Third, by blending personal and academic writing styles to develop multiple voices and different subject positions. Fourth, by investigating how physical journeys through architectural spaces work in dialogue with changes in psychic and emotional states. Fifth, by articulating the interactive relationship between writing and designing. Sixth, by examining how responses to specific sites can pattern the form as well as the content of texts, generating new genres for architectural writing based on (auto)biographies, diaries, guidebooks, letters, poems, stories and travelogues.

Taken together, I suggest that these spatialised and situated writing practices have the potential to reconfigure relations between theory and practice, research and design. They can critique existing methodologies by prioritising the poetic and political, ethical and emotional, qualities of interactions between subjects and sites, and the role these play in creating subtle but meaningful propositions that respond to existing conditions and yet aim to imagine beyond them.

The site-writing method departs from the choice of a site to work with, research and investigate, and to respond to. Participants are asked to produce a piece of site-writing as a way of setting up a relationship with their chosen site(s). This can take the form of a piece of prose and/or installation or performative/participatory event documented as an artist's book. This approach explores writing as a form of situated practice, and finds alternative ways of writing architectural history, examining the relation between image and text, different kinds of voice, modes of storytelling, positionality in language, the potential of (auto)biography, and new sites for writing on and off the page.

The site-writing approach finds its roots in my 2006 book *Art and Architecture* which concludes by arguing that since responses to art and architectural works happen *in situ*, we understand them to take place *somewhere*, and that thus criticism itself must be recognised as a form of critical spatial or situated practice. The desire to work with variations in voice to reflect and create spatial distances and proximities between works and texts; artists, writers and readers; became the motivation for a mode of pedagogy and writing practice, which reached one form of culmination in a collection of essays and documentations of text works of my own, produced between 1998 and 2008 which question and perform notions of situatedness and spatiality in critical writing, *Site-Writing* (2011). This pedagogical aspect of site-writing continues to develop through the evolution of the post-graduate teaching module I have led since 2001 (now part of a new MA in Situated Practice), the exhibitions of student work, and international workshops I host – all of which are documented on www.site-writing.co.uk.

References

Rendell, J. (2006). *Art and Architecture: A Place Between*, London: IB Tauris.

Rendell, J. (2011). *Site-Writing: The Architecture of Art Criticism*. London: IB Tauris.

Further Reading

Rendell, J. (2020). Sites, Situations, and other kinds of Situatedness, B. Roberts (ed), *Expanded Modes of Practice*, Special Issue of *Log*.

Rendell, J. (2020). Marginal modes: Positions-of-architecture-writing. *The Architectural Review* https://www.architectural-review.com/essays/marginal-modes-positions-of-architecture-writing

Bal, M. (2001). Dispersing the gaze: focalization. In *Looking in: The Art of Viewing*, Amsterdam; G and B Arts International,), 41-63.

Soyini Madison, D. (2004). Introduction to Critical Ethnography; Theory and Method. In *Critical ethnography; method, ethics & performance*, London: Sage Publications, 1-16.

Haraway, D. (1988). 'Situated Knowledges: The Science Question in Feminism and the Privilege of Partial Perspective', *Feminist Studies*, v. 14, n. 3, (Autumn 1988) 575-599.

Kwon, M. (2002). 'Genealogy of Site-Specificity,'in *One Place After Another: Site Specific Art and Locational Identity* Cambridge, MA: MIT Press, 11-31.

For a range of projects, see https://site-writing.co.uk/

Site-Writing

Assignment

1
Choose a site – this may be a single site in the city, a building, an artwork, an exhibition, a collection, a small-scale intervention, or a detail. The site may also consist of a pair, series, or constellation of sites connected by a key thematic. The site may also be on-line and/or text based: an edited collection, a journal, a catalogue, a script.

2
Research the site historically, theoretically and culturally.

3
Respond to the site critically and creatively. This response should include words, but these can take the form of text, writing, images or sounds.

4
Take into account the figuration of the writing – how do words you have chosen relate to one another and to other visual and spatial forms (drawings, maps, photographs, sounds, moving images, objects) that are found and made?

5
Relate the writing to the site not only conceptually but also formally – in other words, take into account the structure, style, and language of the writing as well as its content.

6
Consider the writing's spatial relation to the site: is your site-writing a direct insertion into a site, do you intend others to interact it with live, or is it positioned at a distance (in time, in space)? Consider extending writing's genres: pamphlets, posters, scores, travelogues, guidebooks, instructions, letters.

7
Consider your and the work's situatedness: if you are making a film, is this to be shown on the internet, in a cinema, in a gallery, projected onto a wall on the street; will the sound play loud, or will the audience by invited to wear headphones, to sit/stand etc.?

8
Produce a print-ready document (such as a pdf.) which is to be conceived as a work (an artist's book) which may also be a documentation of an installation or live event.

assignment

Stacking Narratives

From *Dérive* to Archive Fever

method

Luís Santiago Baptista
Universidade Lusófona de Humanidades e Tecnologias, Lisboa / ESAD, Caldas da Rainha

Our knowledge of reality takes place through direct experience of space and through the action of the memory that supports it. Any fieldwork project therefore has to cross the experience with the archive; the subjective perception of reality with the multiple representations of places. The '*Dérive*/Archive Fever' method intentionally explores this complex relationship, seeking to individualise these two dimensions of our understanding of places, distinguishing spatial practice from archival research. The objective is to displace the conventional and familiar assumptions of our relationship with places, enhancing the opening of alternative narratives.

We understand space in the broad sense, as presented by Henri Lefebvre (1991) in *La Production de l'Espace*, through his conceptual triad between "perceived space," "conceived space," and "lived space," crossing a phenomenological basis with a more political and social critical analysis. This conception implies that, "We should have to study not only the history of space, but also the history of representations, along with that of their relationships – with each other, with practice, and with ideology," (Lefebvre, 1991, p. 42). Space is thus understood in the intersection between the ways of appropriation of space by a community, the conceptions of those who design and build it, and the symbolic systems that give structure to a given society or culture; and so at the confluence between practices, models and representations materially manifested in the places we inhabit.

The first phase comprises the experience of a specific place. Without much prior knowledge, the spatial qualities of the place are revealed through attentive and curious experience, seeking to apprehend and understand its structure and environment. The interpretation of place is carried out in a free and intuitive way, in line with the situationist *dérive*. As Guy Debord stated, "*Dérive* is defined as a technique of swift passage through varied environments [...] indissolubly linked with the recognition of the effects of psychogeographic nature, and with the assertion of a ludic-constructive comportment" (Mcdonough, 2009, p. 78). The experience is motivated by this performativity of space in the sense of momentary liberation from its usual con-

Journey into the Invisible was a project curated by Luís Santiago Baptista and Maria Rita Pais between 2016 and 2019, divided in three phases: an excursion (10-12 June 2016; left photo: Nuno Cera), an exhibition (Thalia Theatre, Lisbon, July–August 2017; right photo: José Carlos Duarte), and a book (Baptista & Pais, 2019).

straints and conditions. The result is the revelation of space beyond its horizon of functional, ideological and symbolic determination.

The second, archival phase reintroduces the multiple historical representations of the place, whether real or fictional, material or intangible, artistic or documental. Conducted in libraries or archives or even through digital search engines, research must collect and collate textual and iconographic information, deliberately expanding the field of analysis and confusing the traditional differentiation of archival material. Taking into account the memory of the previous spatial experience, the various archival representations must be reconstituted in alternative narratives about the place, both historical and material as well as fictional and imaginary. The summoning of the archive oscillates between extremes: on the one hand, history as a plural and fragmentary construction – as presented by historian, Manfredo Tafuri through the defence of the displacement inherent to its constant and endless "deconstructive and reconstructive labour" (Tafuri, 1987, p. 8); and on the other hand, the fictional reconstruction of reality, inspired by Salvador Dali's "paranoid-critical" method, defended by Rem Koolhaas in *Delirious New York*, as "the fabrication of evidence for unprovable speculations and the subsequent grafting of this evidence on the world, so that the 'false' fact takes its unlawful place among the 'real' facts." (Koolhaas, 1994, p. 241). Between the deconstructive and the delirious, the experiential and archival method of stacking narratives about places enhances their performative and significant opening while revealing their social, political and cultural determination.

References

Baptista, L.S., Pais, M.R. (Eds.). (2019). *Viagem ao Invisível: Espaço, Experiência, Representação*. Lisboa: Purga.

Koolhaas, R. (1994 [1978]). *Delirious New York*. New York: The Monacelli Press.

Lefebvre, H. (1991 [1974]). *The Production of Space*. Malden-USA / Oxford-UK.

McDonough, T. (ed.) (2009). *The Situationists and the City*. London / New York: Verso.

Tafuri, M. (1987 [1980]). *The Sphere and the Labyrinth: Avant-Gardes and Architecture from Piranesi to the 1970s*. Cambridge-Massachusetts / London-UK: The MIT Press.

Assignment

1
Select a specific place or building to do the exercise.

2
Visit the place or building in dérive mode exploring its performativity and spatial qualities.

3
Research for textual and iconographical material in libraries, archives, and digital search engines.

4
Produce new architectural or urban narratives with the collected material in a deconstructive or delirious manner.

5
Revisit the place and repeat the process if necessary.

assignment

Storying Stories

Socio-spatial practices and their meaning

method

Dalia Milián Bernal
School of Architecture, Tampere University

> VM: I don't know what you asked me at the beginning, I just started talking.
>
> ***DMB: The question was, how did 1319.TreceDiecinueve start?***
>
> VM: It started when we returned from Barcelona.
> (Excerpt from narrative interview with Verónica Mansilla, 23 January 2018.)

'Storying stories' is a method whereby the (urban) researcher seeks out stories of personal experience both by means of and within qualitative, in-depth and/or narrative interviews and then generates stories out of those experiences (McCormack, 2004). Storying stories is an analytic tool employed to analyse qualitative interviews and it is particularly useful for research that aims to understand a process and/or an individual's actions and experiences as well as the meanings the individual confers to such actions and experiences.

Coralie McCormack (2004) put forth this method within feminist, postmodern, and qualitative research, recognising and valorising situated and subjective stories of personal experience as legitimate sources of knowledge. While McCormack's research does not focus on the spatial dimension of people's lives, this method can also be employed to explore and understand people's socio-spatial practices, the meaning they confer to such practices, and the way individuals experience, engage with, appropriate, and transform urban places.

There are three stages to McCormack's storying stories. The first stage is to conduct at least one in-depth, qualitative and/or narrative interview of personal experience designed to elicit long narrations and/or storytelling. The interview (or interviews) must then be transcribed verbatim. Transcribing the interviews and re-listening to them are already considered the initial procedures of the analytical process. In the second stage, the researcher will construct an interpretative story comprised of a beginning, middle and end (this is the storying process). This process is divided into two parts: composing the story's middle and then completing the interpretative story with a beginning and end. To compose the story's middle, the researcher seeks stories within long stretches of narration found in one interview. McCormack follows Gabriele Rosenthal's (1993) four narrative processes (stories, description, argumentation, and theorising) to locate the narrations, and William Labov's model (abstract, orientation, complicating action, evaluation, result or resolution, coda) (Kim, 2016; Riessman, 2008) to locate the stories. However, the researcher can decide to employ other narrative and story structures, since these structures may vary depending on language and culture. Once stories are located, these are given titles which are then temporally ordered. Text is then added to these titles to re-construct the stories. These stories make up the middle of the story. The second step consists of completing the story with a beginning and an ending and composing an epilogue that reflects on the interpretative story. In urban studies, the beginning of the interpretative story may include other information that helps contextualise the story and orient the reader to the story's middle. The information may be collected from sources other than the research participant's story and include other spatial dimensions.

In the third stage, the researcher will compose a narrative from personal experience. This stage is relevant for longitudinal research that conducts interviews with one research participant at different stages of their lives. The personal experience narrative is composed by ordering temporally the participant's interpretative stories and by adding an epilogue that reflects on the personal experience narrative.

I have employed this method in research that aims to understand why people appropriate abandoned urban spaces with their bodies, materially transform them with little resources and a few tools, and provide them new uses, often unleashing other processes beyond the locale and of broader societal value (Milián Bernal, 2022).

References

Kim, J.-H. (2016). *Understanding Narrative Inquiry: The Crafting and Analysis of Stories as Research.* SAGE Publications, Inc. https://doi.org/10.4135/9781071802861

McCormack, C. (2004). Storying Stories: a narrative approach to in-depth interview conversations. *International Journal of Social Research Methodology*, 7(3), 219–236. https://doi.org/10.1080/13645570210166382

Milián Bernal, D. (2022). Narratives of Appropriation: Abandoned Spaces, Entangled Stories, and Profound Urban Transformations. *Writingplace: Journal for Architecture and Literature*, 6, 69–89.

Riessman, C.K. (2008). *Narrative Methods for the Human Sciences.* SAGE Publications, Inc.

Rosenthal, G. (1993). Reconstrucion of life stories. Principles of selection in generating stories for narrative biographical interviews. In R. Josselson & A. Lieblich (Eds.), *The Narrative Study of Lives Volume 1*, 59–91.

Assignment

Part I. Conduct a short narrative interview with someone you know.

1
Ask for permission to record the short interview.

2
Ask the interviewee to tell you what they know about the neighbourhood they live in.

3
Ask them to tell you the story of when and why they decided to move to that neighbourhood.

Part II. Locating stories

4
Re-listen to the recording. (There's no need to transcribe for the purpose of this assignment.)

5
Locate stories within the narration. You can use Labov's model:
a   Abstract: a summary of the story. It may use words such as: 'Well, it all started when…'
b   Orientation: person's description of the place, or who he/she was with, and the time.
c   Complicating action: this is the plot, an event, a turning point.
d   Evaluation: the interviewee makes sense of the meaning of his/her actions.
e   Result or resolution
f   Coda: the narration goes back to the present.

6
What did you learn about your narrator's story that was surprising? What did you learn about the relationship between your narrator and the neighbourhood he/she lives in? What information about the context was revealed in your narrator's story?

7
Write a short story with a clear beginning, middle and end to report back the answers to the questions above.

Streaming the Urban
A polyphonic exercise

method

Alexandra Purnichescu
Independent researcher, Bucharest

The stream-of-consciousness method draws on the analogous psychologically-originated narrative device meant for exploring, analysing and revealing the inner, subjective, personal, and individualised city by making known the anonymous urban voices. It is through thoughts, words, associations, gestures, and actions that both fictional characters and city dwellers project themselves onto the places they (wish to) inhabit. The city is seen as a written discourse and the viewpoints of the city exponents help make manifest and prospect the interior/subjective city. Based on the experiences of its different inhabitants, this technique aims to analyse the reflection of mental structures and perceptions on the ever-changing urban tissue. The objective of the method is to document, collect, and classify individual evidence of the space perception of a given urban territory. Members of a local community, commuters and/or daily travellers give feedback in participatory sessions. The resulting insights and data may prove useful in rethinking the space, approaching different aesthetic and functional aspects, and improving urban well-being.

The method benefits from the contributions of a typical representative of the technique, the *flâneur*, who develops a strong bond with the city through observation and interaction. The writer-*flâneur* takes part in a process of urban reaction while in search of individual meaning and memory. *Flâneurs* – both contemporary and past – contemplate, take notes and photos, sketch, make connections, and classify. A certain pedagogy of observation is necessary to develop a hermeneutic of seeing, hence the intervention of visual artists and other theoreticians. Assuming a mole's perspective, one explores the city's alleys, passageways, and hidden places in an attempt to read each other's written cities. At the same time, one shifts from a private voice to a public one in order to capture the momentary, the accidental, and the neglected.

The personal paths and routes taken by city inhabitants outline a subjective, emotional iconography of the city as the constant and unpredictable flow of ideas and impressions. These ideas and impressions retrieve the past reality and memory of the city, thus making way for an enriched contemporary consciousness. This may in turn lead to a reconciliation of the various historical and cultural layers of the city's evolution, architecture and community life in the context of the decline and degradation of contemporary space. Similar to *Denkbilder* (thought-images), the resulting miniature city-portraits, which encapsulate the urban experiences, are perceived through the eyes and thought patterns of passers-by.

The method thus deals with the production of unique, individualised spatial recollections, patterns and configurations mirrored in oral discussions, written texts, and visual manifestations. Once these patterns are put together, they collide, overlap, mix and influence each other to generate an encompassing, often divergent reading key of that particular city, drawing on what can be called: the common vision of the community inhabiting and/or crossing that particular space.

The method is potentially applicable to different urban contexts since it is accessible, flexible, spontaneous and sincere in nature; besides, it is rooted in fundamental mental processes and involves the individuals' inherent connection to the inhabited space. The aesthetic experience will also serve to assign meaning to public spaces. Streaming urban spaces is getting closer to the reality of the city as seen in a time continuum on a (un)conscious level in a polyphonic exercise. It is meant to shape a more favourable and human-scaled city while capitalising on the spiritual and urban material heritage.

Further reading

Cohn, D. (1978). *Transparent Minds: Narrative Modes for Presenting Consciousness in Fiction*. Princeton: Princeton University Press.

Featherstone, M. (1998). The 'Flâneur', the City and Virtual Public Life. *Urban Studies*, vol. 35, no. 5/6, 909–25.

Friedman, M. (1955). *Stream of Consciousness: A Study in Literary Method*, New Haven: Yale University Press.

Gilloch, G. (2002). *Walter Benjamin, Critical Constellations*. Cambridge: Polity.

James, W. (1890). *The Principles of Psychology*. Volume 1. New York: Henry Holt and Company,

Schreiber, E.J. (1996). "Dream Visions and Stream-of-Consciousness: The Conscious and Unconscious Search for Meaning". In *Journal of the Fantastic in the Arts*, vol. 7, no. 4 (28), 4–15.

Assignment

1
Students choose an urban place they are strongly emotionally attached to, that holds a particular individual importance and/or that contains personal memories, which they have not visited in a long time.

2
Through the eyes of the *flâneur*, the revisitation of the place will provide opportunities for noting the physical and the nonmaterial changes and transformations: the built environment, with the possible restoration, demolition and urban development works, the urban plan, the functions, the overall atmosphere and spirit of the place, the way people (both residents and passers-by) relate to the place and, last but not least, the way the student currently perceives it.

3
Students actively interact with the place by collecting data and discussing with the inhabitants (e.g. free talks and/or mini-interviews and previously prepared questionnaires).

4
The resulting data is later analysed with architects, focused on trying to understand the place in terms of potential, evocative/symbolic capacity, development possibilities and relationship with its inhabitants.

5
Adding to the overall insight, students draw an aerial perspective of the selected space and a detail of choice, visually overlapping memory and the present moment while pinpointing similarities and differences in a both affective and affectionate enterprise meant to reconcile the city of memory and the contemporary city.

assignment

Surveying with the PlaceMaker Method

Marichela Sepe
Sapienza Università di Roma

The complex-sensitive approach studies urban places in all their complexity; it is sensitive because it is open to all the stimuli provided by such places and seeks to identify and represent elements linked to features which are both perceptual and objective, permanent and transitory. The main method of analysis and design that follows this kind of approach is called 'PlaceMaker' (Sepe, 2013). It considers places from multiple points of view and with different but compatible tools. The main products are two final complex maps; one of analysis and one of design: these represent place identity and project interventions in order both to establish a dialogue with local people, and support planners and administrators in sustainable urban construction and conversion.

The analysis phases are useful to describe and write places. One of these analysis phases is of particular utility in describing place, it consists of five surveys: denominative, perceptive, graphical, photographic and video. The first (denominative) survey aims to collect data concerning the categories chosen in preparing the database, and is related to constructed elements, natural elements, transportation modes, and to people. This survey is called denominative because it deals with naming the things that one sees. The operation of naming urban features is useful both to identify buildings and monuments which are in some way already codified, and to name those elements and places which, though not precisely defined, contribute to constructing the urban landscape and to forming place identity. The second survey is the perceptual one. It covers sensory perceptions such as smell, sound, taste, tactile and visual sensations, and overall perception; focusing on location, type, quantity and quality. Next comes the graphical survey which consists of sketching the places concerned; the sketches will represent the area in question from a visual-perceptual standpoint and will be supported by written notes as required. Finally, photo and video surveys of the whole study area are then carried out, focusing more on the recording of facts than on providing an interpretation of the places.

The main users targeted by the method and software are urban designers, planners and administrators, while a simplified form of the complex map is available for citizens, place users, and visitors. Regarding administrators and city planners, PlaceMaker enables them

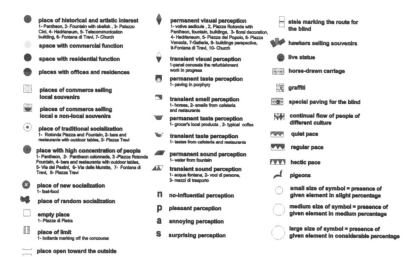

PlaceMaker method, legend for a map of the place identity of the Trevi-Pantheon path in Rome, Italy. (Image by the author).

to understand, in the framework of the planning process, the potentials and problems relating to any given place, how the place itself is perceived by its users and residents, and what the possible actions are in order to improve its quality. The maps enable the collection of analytical data on the place and data for project design purposes. These may be used for specific purposes, including: to redefine the identity and image of a place in regeneration operations; to assess the compatibility of any activity with its identity; to gauge whether the recovery of previous businesses or activities in case of post-disaster reconstructions are still in line with current demands; and to enhance the identity resources in order to sustainably render a place more attractive for visitors. As for the citizens, PlaceMaker enables them to garner a deeper understanding of their city's identity, and feel stronger ties to it so that they will protect and safeguard it or play a proactive role by proposing improvements to administrators and participating in planning choices. Lastly, tourists and place users will find that the map provides an insight into the city that goes beyond mere identification of major landmarks and captures the complexity of place identity, including its tangible and intangible elements, both permanent and temporary. Experiments were carried out in Europe, the United States and Japan in areas of historical interest which were emblematic for the city in question.

References

Carmona, M., Heath, T., Oc, T., Tiesdell, S..(2010, 2nd edition). *Public places-Urban spaces*, Oxford: Architectural Press.

Cullen G. (1961). *Townscape. London*: The Architectural Press.

Lynch, K. (1960). *The image of the city*, Cambridge Mass.: The MIT Press.

Rose G. (1995). Place and identity: a sense of place. In Massey D., Jess P. (Eds.) A Place in the world? *Place, cultures and globalization*, Oxford: Open University/Oxford University Press.

Example/application

Sepe M. (2013). *Planning and Place in the City, mapping place identity*. London, New York: Routledge.

Assignment

The five surveys of the PlaceMaker method are: denominative, perceptive, graphical, photographic and video.

1

Create different types of data-bases to contain the different types of data collected: the denominative and perceptive (through words), the graphical (signs and symbols), the photographic (fixed images), and video (moving images) surveys.

2

Decide what the categories of elements to analyse are, which are particularly connected to the urban events and the corresponding measurement parameters. Moreover, it is necessary to establish which days are the most significant and the most appropriate time slices for surveys.

3

Pursue the five surveys, bearing in mind that each of them, taken singly, is not able to give a complete idea of the place. Only when all the data collected during the five surveys are combined is it possible to have comprehensive information on the elements of the place in nominal and perceptual terms, of a sort that does not emerge from traditional analysis.

4

The output of the five surveys is a map collating the results obtained from each.

assignment

Tailoring Ethnography

(Co-)Present cognition in public realm research

Alasdair Jones
Department of Geography and Global Systems Institute, University of Exeter

Public realm ethnography (Jones, 2021) is an approach developed for studies that take the setting of the public realm– and its socio-spatial qualities – as the "focus rather than the locus" (Hannerz, 1980, p.3) of research. The approach was developed in relation to two key features of public life as conceptualised by Amin (2008), namely 'situated multiplicity' and co-presence with strangers (left photo). It was also developed in response to a recurrent observation in public space research that public spaces are often characterised by an absence of social activities in which the public can participate (right photo).

Critically, these qualities undermine the utility of 'participant observation' for public realm research: first, because of the multiplicity and fluidity of activities to participate in (and of co-presence of others to participate in activities with), and second, because, at other times, of the complete absence of activities to participate in and of others to interact with.

In light of these limitations, I specify an alternative data collection method: *(co-)present cognition*. Herein, data are collected through emphases on physical (co-)presence in the field (rather than on participation in social groups or activities), on multisensorial cognition, and on reflexivity.

Procedurally, '(co)-present cognition' involves overlapping fieldwork tasks. First, having developed a (often exploratory and provisional) research question, the researcher immerses themselves in a public realm setting – spending long periods there (sampling for different time periods) to familiarise themselves with it. The researcher then collects direct observational data (in fieldnotes and/or using audio-visual recording equipment) in a sequential and iterative way, shifting from, i) more systematised observations of (predetermined sectors of) the setting, to ii) more focused and immersive observations of particular social phenomena of interest.

The impracticality of participant observation for ethnographic studies of public realm settings: (i) 'situated multiplicity' and co-presence with strangers on London's South Bank (left-hand image) and (ii) social inactivity on London's South Bank ([right-hand image). (Photographs by the author).

Throughout, '(co)-present cognition' involves being attentive to non-visual sensory aspects of the setting. It is also characterised by an emphasis on reflexivity; being attentive (in your fieldnotes) to your own uses of, participation in, and responses to the setting and its constituent public life.

References

Amin A. (2008). Collective culture and urban public space. *City* 12(1), 5-24.

Hannerz U. (1980). *Exploring the City: Inquiries Toward an Urban Anthropology.* New York: Columbia University Press.

Jones, A. (2021). Public realm ethnography: (Non-)participation, co-presence and the challenge of situated multiplicity. *Urban Studies* 58(2), 425-440.

Assignment

1

Guided by the questions below, spend time in a public realm setting of interest, taking care to visit it at different times of the day and to think about its spatial qualities and how these mediate and/or are mediated by the social uses of the setting.
- What is the role of different sorts of borders/boundaries in the setting?
- How are borders/boundaries of various kinds signified to users of public space, and for what perceptible purposes?

2

Use fieldnotes to collect your data, but think about the different sorts of multi-sensory and other data (e.g. digital and visual traces/artefacts) you can collect to help you answer the questions above.

3

Start your fieldwork by collecting systematised observations from a fixed vantage point – systematically observe where people congregate, what they do, their patterns of movement etc. – to get a broad sense of a range of socio-spatial border phenomena.

4

Then move to more exploratory and directed observations of specific border/boundary phenomena revealed in step (2). For example, the way a particular social practice creates temporary borders. This phase of (co)-present cognition is often mobile, perambulatory, and immersive.

5

Ensure that your fieldnotes are both descriptive (what you see and sense) and reflexive (how you respond to what you see and sense).

6

Return iteratively to the set questions, using them to guide your fieldwork practice.

7

Write up a 2-3 page provisional account of what you found out, linking your findings to excerpts from your fieldnotes.

8

As you write up your account, you may want to consider the following:
- How were you able to account for your own experience of the field in your fieldnotes?
- If you were to employ (co-)present cognition more fully, what sorts of sensorial data might you collect and analyse (and how)?

assignment

Transcribing the City as a Character

Sophie van Riel, Christ & Gantenbein
Italo de Vroom, INBO
Willie Vogel, Studio Inscape / Delft University of Technology

A method to enforce the strong connection between storytelling and architecture is by constructing stories about mid-sized cities as a fictional character. The built environment stores and conveys forms of knowledge and experiences that together form a web of stories. Already since the 1980's, architectural schools such as the AA in London have investigated the stories and narratives in activities and movements of citizens. Students published the visualisations of movements in beautiful drawings for NATØ (Narrative Architecture Today). The technique of personification of places was used in early modern society by writers such as Walter Benjamin (1892-1940) and James Joyce (1882-1941)(Malone, T. 2018). In their writings, the characters present the now, and give "flashing signs of future potentials" (Duffy and Boscagli, 2011, p. 12). For example, the Parisian arcades described by Benjamin were not only a new typology made possible by the innovations in steel and glass but held many layers of information of both past and future. The new glass shopping windows made the imagination come alive.

Through observing detailed spatial aspects of our environment, specific aspects of urban places can be distinguished, and lead to an understanding of the city as a character. Transcribing such a collection of observed urban aspects into a personification allows the researcher to create poetic images that are not static but develop in numerous directions, to create space for subtleties and to address pressing issues. Transcription is more than merely translating or describing what one sees, as the act of transcribing from one register to another may generate new qualities and potentialities (Havik, 2014, p. 99). In the case of personifying a place, the transcription could open a new narrative frame to which people can relate more easily (Jamieson, 2017, p. 90). A good example of an architect who works with transcription is Bernard Tschumi. In his project Joyce's Garden, Tschumi studies the specific setting of places to reorganise the movement and actions that exist between them. These movements and actions are transcribed to a point grid, functioning as a mediator between the program itself and the architectural texts.

Our proposed method includes more than movement. Also interviews, physical surroundings and historical facts are included when transcribing a character as a way to come towards a rich analysis of a place. The transcribed character can raise questions regarding the appearance, behaviour, and the dreams the place wants to fulfil. Therefore, using this technique can also be relevant in a dialogue with citizens, urban planners, architects, and policy makers. Furthermore, when describing a range of cities as characters, they can relate to each other as in a story or a play. In this manner, relationships between cities can be imagined within a larger geographical area. We have to acknowledge that the method would be most useful in small and mid-size cities, as larger cities already contain such diverse characters that a transcription would either be impossible, or result in a schizophrenic character of the city.

Through transcribing the city as a character, places can come alive in the mind of the maker and consumer, writer and reader, or architect and user. To understand cities as characters gives citizens the opportunity to create a sense of rootedness or provides architects with the opportunity to incorporate a sense of place in their designs.

References

Duffy, E., & Boscagli, M. (2011). Introduction: Joyce, Benjamin and Magical Urbanism. In *Joyce, Benjamin and Magical Urbanism*, Brill, 7-29.

Havik, K.M. (2014). *Urban literacy: A descriptive approach to the experience, use and imagination of place*. Rotterdam: nai010 publishers.

Jamieson, C. (2017). *Natø: Narrative architecture in postmodern London*. London: Taylor & Francis.

Malone, T. (2018, April 20). *City as Character, Getting lost in the text-cities of Joyce, Döblin, and Dos Passos*. Lamps Quarterly. https://www.laphamsquarterly.org/roundtable/city-character

Further reading

Van Riel, De Vroom, Vogel. (2019, June). *Someone//Somewhere - the European Union, a Home for so many Differences*. Graduation project TU Delft https://repository.tudelft.nl/islandora/object/uuid%3Adfd031aa-3712-41a3-a1ef-eb58c08281ac?collection=education

Transcribing the City as a Character

Assignment

1
To start off well prepared, collect as much relevant information (such as its history, economy, culture, and more) you need about the city which you are going to visit.

2
Pick one or more important city square(s) that you want to visit. Think about the square as the navel of the city - the square you choose to visit must be relevant to many different groups of people.

3
While on site, document the architecture, activity and people. Make photos of the buildings, their details and the design of the public space in general. Use video to document the activity on the square. What are the main dynamics/activities – which sounds belong to it, at which time of the day do they take place, etc.? In addition, try to interview a handful of people. Ask them about the relevance of the square and their reasons for living in that city, the parts they really like and the things they would like to improve – dreams and potentials.

4
When done, summarise the gathered information in place (where), act (what), and actors (who). This is the first step for writing your character.

5
Make a short description of the place as if it is a typical character. Think about:
a. Sex: he/she/neutral
b. age
c. clothes
d. family/friends/relatives (which other characters are related?)
e. activity (daily routine)

6
Lastly, to finish the writing, think about the development of the character. Is there something specific that this character wants to fulfil? What will their future be like? What do they dream of? What do others write about the city?

7
Make your character come alive! Compare your outcome with others, are there similarities, contradictions? Can your character start a discussion?

assignment

Transforming through 'Active Space'

Super site specific explorations and activation of 'spaces of possibilities'

Jens Brandt
School of Architecture, Tampere University

> *We focus attentively on the new field, the urban, but we see it with eyes, with concepts, that were shaped by the practices and theories of industrialisation, [which] is therefore reductive of the emerging reality* (Lefebvre, 2003, p. 29)

'Active Space' is a highly structured method that combines elements from participatory performance, pervasive games and psychogeography. The overall goal is to work in socially produced spaces – such as neighbourhoods, street corners, villages etc. – to foster and nurture political or democratic transformations.

Transformation is here understood as, 'changing the way to change,' that challenges the concepts shaped by the past (industrialisation as in the Lefebvre quote above). By exploring an embodied experience of (body) space, the method aims to discover spaces of possibilities, a sensation of radical openness that can spark the motivation to act. This drives a rhythm that moves between the verbal and non-verbal of socially-produced spaces and creates a signifying process that empowers language for action.

A 'gameplay' uses representations (such as images and text) to go beyond representation. Inspired by the concept of instruction pieces in the field of performance, it visualises how actions unfold over time that produces an 'Active Space'. This can be seen as a meta methodology for many settings such as a 48-hour camp, a 5-day exploration or a semester course. In this case, 'Active Space' is used in a very simple (off-site) procedure that can be done alone.

'Active Space' has two main components: spaces, and movements (actions). These components involve the following three spatial aspects: first, *Body Space*, which is non-verbal, sensory and intuitive; second, *Social Space*, which focuses on language and social

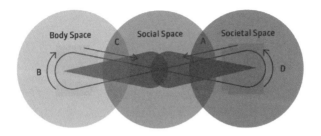

The main components of Active Space.

interaction; and third, Societal Space, which relates to the technological, legal, economic, and scientific. The four movements that drive the rhythm are:

A Gameplay: Set of actions that unfold in time and space; exit the repetitive inertia of societal space.
B Exploration: Involving all senses to explore what is there and how does it feel.
C Agenda: Developing a common vocabulary and collaboration on an agenda (goals).
D Action: How to achieve the agenda involving the societal conditions for actions.

References

Lefebvre, H. (2003). *The urban revolution*. Minneapolis, MN: University of Minnesota Press.

Lilliendahl Larsen, J., & Brandt, J. (2018). Critique, creativity and the co-optation of the urban: A case of blind fields and vague spaces in Lefebvre, Copenhagen and current perceptions of the urban. *Urban Planning*, 3, 52-69.

Assignment

**Body space
Peripheral perception:**

1
Close your eyes and do a sensory scan of the relation between your body and the world:
a. Feel your skin and be aware of the sensation of touch. Sense how you touch the ground/seat as part of the gravity that pulls us towards the Earth.
b. Take a deep breath. Smell the air and imagine how the oxygen is produced by plants and trees all around the world.
c. Listen to the sounds. Pay attention to how the space itself sounds by listening, for example to the voices from the street. Alternatively, make a sound to hear the space.

**Body space
Spaces of Possibilities (SOP):**

2
Let go of the individual senses and explore how the whole experience of the situation feels.

3
Move your attention to an experience of a situation that made you feel free and able to act. Activate a spatial imagination that gives you the feeling of being there.

4
Keep that feeling in mind as a motivation or energy for the following step.

Social Space:

5
Begin to add words and name the feelings that drive your actions/movements. How would you describe it to others?

6
Find words that describe a set of goals for the movements (actions).

Societal Space:

7
Describe the relevant societal context for the movements; what are the problems and possibilities?

8. Produce a scenario for how to act in this context to achieve the goals.

assignment

Uncannying the Ordinary ...with Cortázar

Esteban Restrepo Restrepo
École Nationale Supérieure d'Architecture de Paris-La Villette

Julio Cortázar is a well-known Argentinian writer who lived in Paris in the second half of the 20th century where he wrote the most of his work, characterised by the introduction of fantastic elements and situations within the everyday life, blurring the limits between fiction and reality - this categorial binarism was unacceptable for him.

One of his most famous works is *Historias de Cronopios y Famas* (Cronopios and Famas), composed of four narrative experiments, including the *Manual de Instrucciones* (The Instruction Manual), where he takes and decontextualises the form and the aim of extremely technical and practical texts that explain (for dummies) how to use objects, machines or household appliances, and apply them 'literally' to some unexpected and anodyne situations, that, one could think, do not need to be explained or 'instructed' because of their obvious use. Thus, he creates manuals of instructions on how to cry, on how to kill ants in Rome, on how to wind up a clock, on how to climb a staircase, among others.

What Cortazar tries to question and challenge in his work is, precisely the automatism of our everyday actions and gestures, our everyday use of objects and spaces, making of them strange and fantastic by means of detailed and serious descriptions, as if it was the first time we use these objects and spaces or undertake these actions. Cortázar makes uncanny the precepts of our reality and/or makes us strangers to that reality, putting us in a reflexive, inventive and re-creative situation.

Nevertheless, actions and gestures, objects and spaces, are not the only entities to be treated as strangers; the body itself (its parts, its forms, its possibilities of movement) is treated as an unfamiliar tool that we need to learn how to use (again).

Cortázar's descriptions give back consciousness to the unconscious. Stepping aside from a very familiar situation for a certain amount of time in order to make its obviousness disappear, the text brings (back) that situation, unavoidably, to the realm of the extraordinary, even to the realm of the fantastic.

However, we can find in Cortázar's work some devices that operate in exactly the opposite way we just announced: when the odd tries to become or to cohabitate with the familiar, as is the case of the short story *Bestiario* (Bestiary), where a family and a tiger try to live together within a house. They create a precise routine that prevents them from meeting in the same room at the same time which could lead them to succumb. It is a beautiful paradox and a metaphor of a tolerant and synchronic way of living with the unknown, with the 'differ-ent'.

Cortázar's procedure, that we call 'Uncannying the Ordinary,' could be used as a creative method while writing, conceiving, and experiencing places. It is through a still and patient practice of observation, that we could consider as a sort of hypnosis, that we can release objects, forms, actions, uses, functions, habits etc. from their banality, from their repetition, from their moral immanence, and lead them to a state of innovation by revealing their (Freudian) *unheimlich*, their mystery, their singularity, their firstness.

References

Cortázar, J. (1962). Manual de Instrucciones. In *Historia de Cronopios y Famas*. Buenos Aires: Minotauro.

Cortázar, J. (1969). The Instruction Manual. In *Cronopios and Famas*, translated by Paul Blackburn New York: Pantheon Books.

Cortázar, J. (1951). Bestiario. In *Bestiario*. Buenos Aires: Editorial Sudamericana.

Cortázar, J. (1967). Bestiary. In *End of the Game and Other Stories*, translated by Paul Blackburn. New York: Pantheon Books.

Uncannying the Ordinary

Assignment

1
Look around and focus on the most banal object you see, whether you are in a private or a public space. It could be a door, a window, a bench, a lamp, a sign, whatever you choose will suffice.

2
Keep looking at your object, take your time, stare at it, no thoughts are needed (at the moment); just a deep and still observation.

3
Interrogate the object. Start by evident questions like what its shape and colour is, what materials is it made of, how it is used, by whom, etc.

4
Reflect on how the space (and the world) you are in would be if the object did not exist.

5
Keep staring at your object until it starts to look weird (because you are not used to looking at it that much, and much less so to interrogate it), until you visualise it as something extraordinary, as something that is not immanent or natural, as something whose existence is not obvious.

6
Put yourself in the situation of the inventor of the object. How did he/she create it? Following which needs? What technical and aesthetical constraints did he/she take into account? (You can invent your answers.)

7
Now put yourself in the situation of the first person that used the object. Describe the failed attempts before this person used it correctly (you will need to invent your answers).

8
Describe the object and the (right) way to use it to an alien (or to a being, real or imaginary, that has a physiognomy different than a human: an animal, a plant, a bacteria, a ghost).

9
Transcribe the (eventual) reactions that the 'alien' would have after reading your description.

10
Put the object in its context again and describe the 'new perspective' you have on it.

assignment

Walking and Scoring

method

Saskia de Wit
Faculty of Landscape Architecture, Delft University of Technology

Some of the qualities of an urban landscape can only be understood through direct experience: sound, scent, materiality etc. And the most direct way to experience the (urban) landscape is by walking: a multisensory, active interaction with the urban landscape. When walking deliberately, the human body functions as a measuring device, exposing the city as a structure of spaces seen as well as felt, touched, and heard. To understand and make sense of these experiences, a researcher needs a second, interpretive component: a notation technique. Such a notation technique, that can translate and interpret the narrative and spatiotemporal quality of walking and allows for reading the urban landscape as a sequence of events or atmospheres, is the score: the symbolisation of a process, which extend over time (such as a musical score represents a musical composition). The most straightforward score looks like a linear graph, with a horizontal dimension that shows the progress over time, which in the case of a walk is the distance walked in metres, and a vertical dimension that visualises the relative amount of change in sensory quality/quantity.

In the 1960s and 1970s American landscape architect Lawrence Halprin started experimenting with alternative notation techniques for analysis and design. Inspired by the close relationship he had with dance and theatre, the choreography of movement became a key notion for his designs. He invented an ideographic system, using scores to document changes over time, in all fields of human endeavour. Halprin called the type of score that represents human movement in space, 'motation' (Halprin, 1969). However, the scores he invented took the actor as the subject. When we make the urban landscape the subject, we can reverse this technique, and use the actor and his or her actions (walking) as the tool (de Wit, 2018, p. 412).

To explore these experiential qualities of the urban landscape that change as we move through them, a researcher should walk with determination and focus, using each of the different faculties of their own body as a measuring device to record one specific aspect, each of which can be expressed in a score. For example, a first walk could be guided by the eye, with focused attention to the visual scenogra-

Visual-spatial score of the Tofuku-ji temple ensemble (Tokyo, Japan). The score shows how each transition from one area to another is marked by an enclosure, and how the sizes of the spaces become smaller towards the garden. (Images by the author, 2018).

phy of the routing while singling out those elements at eye level that inform the line of movement: views, landmarks, and expansions and contractions of space. These can be represented in a visual score: a sequence of abstracted, perspectival images as informed interpretations of the visual elements as they enter your retina, without interference of your mind and before they become connected by underlying meanings and knowledge (fig. 1). Another walk might focus on the dynamic properties of the ground plane, which can be perceived through ascent and descent, moving left or right, straight ahead, or turning back, factors of the site which influence bodily position, as interpreted by the muscles and the vestibular organ. The locomotion score identifies these properties of the ground that influence the physical act of moving (fig. 2). Closely related is the surface underfoot: the material properties of texture, roughness or smoothness, and details of surface variation. Firm surfaces require little attention to negotiate; the more muscular and vestibular effort they require, the more awareness of one's surroundings they provide. These properties can be related to one another in a surface-underfoot score, with on one end of the scale being smooth and slippery surfaces, and on the other, soft, bumpy, loose, or rocky surfaces. Another walk might be dedicated to the interaction between different sound sources: traffic, human voices, wind, birds etc. which can be registered in an auditory score.

By repeating the same walk, and creating comparable scores for multiple sensory components, you will find that the rhythm, volume, and quality of the different scores interact with each other. And just as a musical composition contains threads of different instruments; scores for the different sensory components can collaborate to communicate the perceivable form of the urban landscape.

Walking and Scoring

References

Halprin, L. (1969). *The RSVP Cycles; Creative processes in the human environment.* New York: George Braziller.

Wit, S.I. de (2018). *Hidden Landscapes. The Metropolitan Garden as a Multi-sensory Expression of Place.* Amsterdam: Architectura & Natura.

Assignment

1

Determine two points of interest at c. 500 metres distance on a map and print the map on A3 paper in black and white. Because you can't zoom in and out on a print, this will allow you to keep a sense of the relative distances. Draw a line that connects the points, using existing paths.

2

Select one sensorial aspect: visual-spatial, locomotive, auditory, etc. (To capture all its detail and finesse it is necessary to focus on one sensorial aspect at a time).

3

Start walking. Walk with a colleague or friend. This will allow you to discuss each moment of change in the quality of visual cues, sounds, and body equilibrium.

4

Use your body as a measuring device: your eyes for noticing view lines, landmarks and panoramas, and widening and compressing of spaces; your ears for differentiating sounds; the muscles in your legs and your vestibular organ for registering level changes and curves and bends in the road, and your feet for the material underfoot. (You could try to walk barefoot, but also when wearing shoes, you'd be surprised how much the surface changes determine your balance once you start paying attention).

5
Mark each observed moment of change on the map. Annotate as much as possible about the quality and the quantity of each change. It might be helpful to use your phone to locate the exact locations. If necessary, adjust your anticipated line.

6
Take photographs to document the moments of change.

7
Once back behind your desk, if necessary, collect (cartographic) information in order to, for example, objectively document locomotive aspects and verify your findings.

8
Draw a linear graph (similar to a musical score). The horizontal dimension shows the distance walked in metres. The vertical dimension describes the perceived changes in the sensory aspect you are researching (e.g. volume of sound, amount of light, height differences, amount of enclosure, roughness of surface underfoot, etc.). Take your time to invent your own set of values for the vertical bar, relevant to the content of the walk. Divide the vertical dimension in equal bars that visualise the relative amount of change in sensory quality/quantity. Use words to describe the range, such as from loud to absent, or from rough to smooth.

9
Use your notes to complete the score by drawing the line that represents your walk, indicating the relation between the horizontal (time) and the vertical (sensory quality) dimension of the graph. The line moves up or down, abrupt or gradually, according to the moments of change you registered. The line can be drawn in different ways, to add information to the score. For example, multiple intertwining lines of different colours for different types of sound, or different line textures to indicate different underfoot textures, etc.

Walking Backwards

Hanna Kahrola
Freelance dance artist, fema collective, Tampere

Walking backwards is stepping forward with one's backside to the moving direction. In backward walking, the soles of the feet may roll from toe to heel, as opposed to walking with one's chest in front, where the heels touch the ground first.

Walking backwards differs markedly from how people generally move through space. However, it offers an embodied way to inquire into, and engage with urban places. Walking backwards slows our body's movements, affecting the way we observe the space around us, perceive our surroundings, and interact with other people. By reversing walking, the landscape left behind (or in front?) is revealed to the walker little by little and the walker can see, with more detail, what has been left behind.

Walking backwards can be considered a form of art and also a meditative experience. According to Aksentijevic (2019), walking backwards improves short term memory, and Koch (2009) argues that walking backwards may enhance thinking. These findings could be relevant to take advantage of when people encounter and interact in urban places, and are in connection with the physical space.

Walking backwards aligns loosely with queer theory, as queer theory aims to deconstruct normative concepts and phenomena. Walking backwards can be considered a method to understand and challenge our own and others' conceptions and attitudes of how to move in and across urban places. Moving differently and/or in opposite directions can help raise questions regarding the function and organisation of space and the deconstruction of norms but also how to facilitate interpersonal encounters. Therefore, walking backwards is a soft but powerful political statement.

When doing backwards walking for the first time, it is recommended that the walker knows the space well beforehand. When one has expertise in the space it may help with experiencing and observing the space in new ways. Regarding choosing the place to walk, it might be easier to walk in a straight line. In case the road bends or there are rises or falls, it allows one to sense the space and its changes even more with their back. In general, it is beneficial to try to use one's back and soles of the feet as strongly sensory parts of the body while walking backwards. The most important would be to relax and slow down the movement a bit as well, so as to enjoy the experience and the possible impact on how one starts to see the urban place and how fellow people react to the action.

Walking backwards is one of the exercises f*ema artist collective* has used during recent times as part of their bodily and performative urban space practice in the mid-sized city of Tampere, Finland. It is part of their artistic practice and it has been world opening for the artists in the collective.

References

Aksentijevic, A., Brandt, K.R., Tsakanikos, E., & Thorpe, M. J. (2019). It takes me back: The mnemonic time-travel effect. *Cognition*, 182, 242–250.

Koch, S., Holland, R.W., Hengstler, M., & van Knippenberg, A. (2009). Body locomotion as regulatory process: stepping backward enhances cognitive control. *Psychological science*, 20(5), 549–550.

Further reading

Butler, J. (1990). *Gender Trouble – Feminism and the Subversion of Identity*. New York: Routledge.

Website of fema artist collective: https://femacollective.weebly.com/

Walking Backwards

Assignment

1

Choose a place to start walking. Then choose a path and direction: for example, a street, a passage or a sidewalk. Maybe it is good to choose an area that is already familiar to you. If you don't want too much of a challenge it is good to choose a path where there are no road crossings. Also, choose the side of the street that permits pedestrians. Decide beforehand where you are going to finish your walk.

2

Start walking backwards. Choose a calm enough pace so that your steps are stable. At times you can look back or you can challenge yourself to sense backwards without watching.

3

Make observations about yourself while walking. Sense how walking backwards feels for you. Do you sense something different in your body compared to walking forwards? What do you sense in your different body parts? Which body part could lead your walking? How could you make walking backwards as easy as possible, bodily? How do you feel socially about walking backwards in an urban place?

4

Make observations about your surroundings while walking. In which way do you see the landscape, the buildings, the lights, the size of the things, the distances, the details and the whole? How does the ground feel under you and the sky above you? How do you hear the sounds?

5

Make observations about other living beings while walking. How do you see other people? How do you think other people see you? Do you maybe get any glances or comments about your walking? How do you react to them? How do other species react to you?

6

Stop walking at the end point, stand still for a moment and reflect a bit on your experience. Which is the most predominant sensation and thought after walking?

7

If you repeat the exercise, make observations if and how the sensations perhaps change at different times. Thus you can also make observations how repetition affects your activity and ownership in the urban place.

assignment

Wandering Aimlessly

Exploration of an unknown city

method

Aleksandar Staničić
Faculty of Architecture and the Built Environment, Delft University of Technology

In order to understand complex spatial and material conditions of reality, the field trip is considered of vital importance to architectural researchers as it allows for the gaining of insight into the specificities of locality (Solnit, 2001). The *in situ* investigation of a sequence of spaces and/or set of trajectories through the city is then the means through which an array of spatial conditions can be encountered that are probably highly contested, and in which spatial practices of inclusion and exclusion take place. When exploring the presence of contemporary territorial conditions, we consider the physical and slow experience of the spatial context around these territories important, but also appreciate the openness that is situated in the aimlessness of wandering through the city as a specific mode of inquiry. Such practice has its theoretical stronghold in the Dadaist concept of flaneur: "enjoying manifestations of the unusual and the absurd, when wandering about the city" (Careri, 2002, p. 119); the situationist psychogeography, which "attempts to investigate the psychic effects of the urban context on the individual" (p. 141); and *dérive*: meaning, to "literally 'drift,' a recreational collective act that aims at defining the unconscious zones of the city" (p. 141).

The particular *raison-d'être* for this way of exploring the city under investigation is three-fold: (a) learning from reality is not limited to the more official, or high-end, side of architecture only – this would constitute a very limited take on the contemporary production of buildings, infrastructures and spaces in our contemporary cities and territories – instead, architects have long since decided to accept all of reality, with all its conflicts, imperfections, idiosyncrasies and inconsistencies, and investigate this reality with some rigor; (b) when accepting the vast expanse of production in contemporary urbanism, landscape architecture, architecture and infrastructural work, one also needs to accept a no-longer pre-determined, biased and singular viewpoint with which to investigate these spatial conditions – a certain distant gaze and postponement of judgement are needed, in order to be able to properly assess the aforementioned spatial conditions; and (c) both the preparation of the field trip and the object under investigation can never be truly anticipated nor known to the fullest. The bodily engagement during the field trip is not only considered vital to be able to draw any insights from the trip and the different localities encountered, but the walking also introduces a moment of surprise and improvisation in the research. This opening up towards the possibility of the un-foreseen is cultivated as the moment in which the true nature of research emerges, namely to be confronted with conditions that are not anticipated and are therefore in need of being re-assessed (Fard and Meshkani, 2015).

The focus of attention in these aimless wanderings is supposed to be the spatial manifestation of ongoing urban transformations, often combined with aggressive infrastructural insertions into the urban and territorial fabric. The intended purpose of these walks, then, is to investigate and map all these hidden forces with the immediacy as well as the precision, factuality and tangibility of being on-the-ground (O'Rourke, 2013). The imagined trajectories through any urban or territorial context should then be based on an initial intent to allow architectural researchers to be confronted with a great variety of spatial conditions. Via the walk, researchers would be traversing locations in the urban fabric where tensions have mounted, conflicting juxtapositions have emerged, and a variety of spatial regimes in the contemporary city have been superimposed. These conditions are consequently to be scanned, charted and mapped, thus investigating the spatial practices that have been woven into the fabric of the city (Kurgan, 2013; Kurgan and Brawley, 2019). The intention of this type of method, therefore, is not to explore singularities (infrastructure, post-conflict conditions, pollution, what have you), but to investigate the overlapping or the superimposition of such different spatial regimes.

References

Careri, F. (2002). *Walkscapes: Walking as an aesthetic practice*. Barcelona: Editorial Gustavo Gili.

Fard, A., Meshkani, T. (Eds.) (2015), *New Geographies 7: Geographies of Information*. Cambridge: Harvard University Press.

Kurgan, L. (2013). *Close Up at a Distance; Mapping, Technology & Politics*. New York: Zone Books.

Kurgan, L., Brawley, D. (Eds.) (2019). *Ways of Knowing Cities*. New York: Columbia University Press.

O'Rourke, K. (2013). *Walking and Mapping; Artists as Cartographers*. Cambridge/London: The MIT Press.

Solnit, R. (2001). *Wanderlust; A History of Walking*. London: Penguin Books.

Wandering Aimlessly

Assignment

1
Open an actual (printed) map and randomly pick a starting point in a city. While you're at it, think about what attracted you to that exact point. Try to imagine desired trajectory/path, but don't think about it too much. Go to that place and start walking.

2
Try to decipher what attracts you to go in certain direction. If you can't decide, come up with some kind of a system. For example, make a left turn every time you see something unusual, unexpected or absurd; make a right turn every time you see a (spatial) conflict. Get lost.

3
Map the perceived walking trajectory on a blank sheet of paper. Create a legend (inventory) of what you see along the way; for example, you can have one set of symbols for apparent causes of spatial conflicts, one for their spatial manifestations, and many others for urban voids, contact zones, threshold spaces, etc. Don't try to make sense of it... yet. Find your way out.

4
If you are working in a group, have all groups overlap their maps to create the "collective" map of the city. Then overlap the collective map with the actual map. Try to identify spatial patterns and establish a connection between physical characteristics of space and its psychological effect on the perceiving body.

Weaving Stories

Finding, telling and coding text(ile)s

Fernando P. Ferreira
Bartlett School of Architecture, University College London

One of the most interesting ways to find something is to discover it or to perceive it by chance or surprisingly. This singular and paradoxical research practice could be taken into account by architects to reappraise their methodologies when interacting with evidence during their researches on contemporary places. Indeed, architects should consider finding stories as a 'pre-condition' in the process of architectural design: one that is less pre-determined and more open to improvisation and unexpected discoveries.

The ancestral textile practice of weaving, as a collaborative and open-ended methodology of finding and storing stories beyond the more analytical, static, or pre-determined approaches to find information in architectural research, could become a practice leading architects to elaborate on new relationships between place, architecture, and storytelling. It is crucial to remember that weaving is one of the most ancient and compelling practices of human communication and information storage (Plant, 1998). Indeed, Kathryn Sullivan Kruger (2001) points out the communicative capacities of textiles, arguing that weaving is one of the earliest forms of 'text'.

To demonstrate how weaving might become an architectural method for finding and storing stories of places in more specific terms, I made myself a practice-based research, developed at Coelima, a textile factory founded in 1922 in Vale do Ave, Portugal. When I began doing research on the factory's history, I soon realised that part of its recent past was missing. Although Coelima has an institutional archive with relevant documentation dated between 1963 and 1989, from a profound economic crisis in 1991 until today few writing records narrate or explain the factory's latest history.

Following this on-site experience and drawing on Adrian Forty's (2001) argument that memory resides in social events rather than crystallised objects, I proposed to enact collective acts of weaving, or micro 'events of the thread' (Albers, 2017), with a group of female former factory workers. The aim was to fill the gaps in the factory's archive and to experiment with weaving on a 'double back strap loom'[1] (figure) as a mode to find and store polyvocal stories relat-

Former Coelima workers weave and store fragments of their stories on a double backstrap loom. They write parts of their stories on paper and weave the paper, storing the words in the cloth. Photograph Fernando P. Ferreira [2020].

ed to Coelima's 1991 post-crisis. During this experience, the acts of weaving followed two phases of discovering and keeping stories. First, weaving was developed freely, without determining goals, as repetitive assemblies of making and listening to stories in the public space around the factory. By repeating the same action with the same audience, bonds of trust were reinforced, language constraints deconstructed, and hesitations of labour's positionalities dismantled. It also allowed the workers to counteract and heal conflicting memories between one another and offered means to explore fragments of their own life at Coelima that remained forgotten, unwritten, and untold by the factory's archive. In a second phase, two processes of storing stories were explored. First, pieces of shared oral stories were printed on paper and woven into the loom (figure 2). Second, the weaving capacities in storing information were tested through coding (Kruger, 2001; Albers; 2017). Many coding forms were experimented with, improvising with different types of knots, numerical notations, colours, and thread materials. For example, one or more textile knots with a particular colour or material created a unique code corresponding to a letter (figure 3). Repeating these codes or 'letters' in specific ways allowed to store and generate words, sentences, or even a story within the cloth. Indeed, if pushed further, weaving coding might become a generative and variable device for designing new forms of language to find, store, and (re)tell stories by and to others.

The story-weaving practice might lead architects to better 'read' and reorganise a place's history and its spatial and social transformations. Indeed, finding stories through weaving can create a site-specific and collaborative 'prescription' (Havik, 2014) to architectural design: a story-based start to catalyse the architect's imagination when called to rethink places such as Coelima or others elsewhere.

Weaving Stories

Note
1 A 'double backstrap loom' comprises two weaving shafts, two warp bars and two shuttles. The particularity of this loom is that to be set up and ready to weave, it always needs the bodies of two persons to tension the warp threads. Therefore, this device only operates with the bodily presence of the other.

References
Albers, A. (2017). *On Weaving: New Expanded Edition*. Princeton: Princeton University Press.

Forty, A. (2002). Introduction. In *The Art of Forgetting*, edited by Adrian Forty and Susanne Kuchler, 1-18. London: Bloomsbury Publishing PLC.

Havik, K. (2014). *Urban Literacy. Reading and Writing Architecture*. Rotterdam: nai010 publishers.

Kruger, K. (2001). *Weaving The Word: The Metaphorics of Weaving and Female Textual Production*. Selinsgrove: Susquehanna University Press.

Plant, S. (2016). *Zeros and Ones: Digital Women and the New Technoculture*. London: Harper Collins Publishers.

Assignment

1
Locate yourself in a public square, a street, or even inside a public building of a place with a certain degree of historical background, where social dynamics and people's fluxes occur with moderate intensity. Observe how people move and interact in the space selected.

2
Use a 'double backstrap' to weave as a solo performative act, a kind of happening that disrupts the people's movements in the selected public space. Remake this happening several times a day or during several days. If you do so, you will become noticed by the local users and agents who pass by. There is a high probability that the local users will stop to observe you weaving, and interactions and conversations will naturally occur.

3
Invite one local user of the selected public space/building to weave with you on the double backstrap loom to incite a site-specific dialogue through making. Weave freely without preconceived goals, accept chance and ask questions to the user while weaving: What is the history of this space/building? How is your relationship with this place? Can you imagine a different future for this place? Is there anything you would like to change?

4
Combine threads, rhythms, and thoughts, in order to activate the user's memories and visions about the place.

5
Repeat the previous weaving as a time-based action over different days with the same user. Language constraints might be dismantled by repeating and weaving collaboratively, bringing unexpected stories, inner perspectives, and subjectivities to the surface.

6
Experiment with the local user with different possibilities for storing the found stories within the woven cloth through two techniques of 'texere' (text + textiles): write & weave or textile coding.

7
In the first technique, you can invite the user to select and write parts of their shared stories on paper and weave the written pieces of paper in the cloth. The result will join threads, paper, and words in one compelling woven piece.

8
In the second technique, you can develop and create with the local user a form of textile code by testing with variations in acts of repetition with different knots, colours, and materials. If you repeat a specific knot in a particular manner, then you might create a code corresponding to a letter or a word. In so doing, you can create a unique textile language collaboratively, where codes for letters, words, and sentences related to the user's story are stored within the woven cloth.

9
Invite other users of the place and repeat the previous tasks with them or bring more 'double backstrap looms' to the space and create an ensemble of collective acts of finding and storing stories through weaving, writing and coding. You might find a rich set of 'polyvocal' stories related to your place. Although these stories might be diverse, situated, ambivalent, social, ethical, political, or even contradictory, they can be seen here as 'thoughts through action' that might offer possibilities for the future of the place you are in.

10
Exhibit this collection of woven artefacts for multiple publics and agents, as a first step to 'read' or 'decode' critically the visions and stories related to the public space or building in which you are placed. These woven stories might become a 'pre-condition' to ignite spatial imagination when designing the space or building's future.

Writing at 1:50

Building stories with words

Anna Ryan Moloney
School of Architecture, University of Limerick

Within architecture and urban design practices, different scales of representation are used to communicate the various ideas and intentions for a proposal: how the project works within its context; how its spaces are organised; how the materials are detailed. The scale of 1:50 shows space, character, light, texture, atmosphere, and despite its distance or remove, there is something about this scale in drawing – whether plan or section or sectional perspective – that comes closest to bringing together in one representation the factors that show how a set of spaces might be experienced when built. It comes closest to placing the viewer of the drawing within the project: the dimension of the body in relation to the space, the material in relation to the body, the light as experienced by the body.

This 'Writing at 1:50' method transposes what is captured by the design scale of 1:50 into the medium of words. It draws heavily on the work of creative writers, in particular writers of fiction, who, like architects and urban designers, construct worlds. Writers must construct three-dimensional space out of the flat space of the page, using only the material of words. Writing at 1:50 is an immersive practice – both for the writer and for the reader. Writing in this way fully involves the writer in observing, communicating the essences of places and spaces, and then likewise fully immerses the reader, through the act of reading, in visualising those places and spaces in an all-encompassing three-dimensional experience. Writers using this method will find subtle ways to engage their readers, and to involve them in this process.

This method of writing at 1:50 can be used in multiple ways: as tool of spatial description, as a tool of spatial analysis, or as tool of site and spatial exploration. In particular, this method of writing can be used as spatial design tool; a way to speculate futures, to test visions, to propose. Writing at 1:50 is simply another form of representation, another tool in the armoury of the designer, working alongside what are considered the more normative or traditional modes of design representations. Any form of representation has its limits and its opportunities. This method of writing can, and will, do something different than the 'work' of a drawing or a model or a photograph. It can communicate spatial sensations that some of the long-standing forms of spatial representation might struggle to capture. It foregrounds place and space as inhabited, emphasising the nature of embodied experience. With this method, care must be taken not to drop into purely factual writing; into a detached voice of an uninvolved observer.

Though not the specific intention of the authors, the 'applications/examples' in the bibliographic references listed here offer various ways of operationalising this method. Three Irish writers – Maeve Brennan's *Long-Winded Lady* columns from the 1960s in New York; Sara Baume's novel *Spill Simmer Falter Wither*, and teenager Dara McAnulty's non-fiction *Diary of a Young Naturalist* – demonstrate written examples of this method of immersive writing of place; highlighting the precision of observation involved in constructing or (re)constructing space-as-experienced, through words. Anna Ryan's essay offers a theoretical discussion of this interest of writing (in) architecture, and Klaske Havik's book offers a number of broader contexts in which this method can be located.

Examples / Applications
Baume, S. (2015). *Spill Simmer Falter Wither*, London: Windmill Books.

Brennan, M. (1998). *The Long-Winded Lady*, Dublin: The Stinging Fly Press.

McAnulty, D. (2020). *Diary of a Young Naturalist*, Dorset: Little Toller Books.

Further Reading
Havik, K. (2014). *Urban Literacy: Reading and Writing Architecture*. Rotterdam: nai010 publishers.

Ryan, A. (2012). Writing Architecture. In Rowley, Ellen and Laroussi, Maxime (Eds.) *Patterns of Thought*, Dublin: Architecture Republic.

Writing at 1:50

Assignment

1

Select your area of interest; your site. Ideally spend time there: where possible, at different times of the day, at different times of the year. And/or take a space, interior or exterior, of your design proposal, whether or not you have yet drawn it.

2

Make careful observation notes of what you see, hear, feel, smell on your site. Take many photographs and possibly make sketches. Look for what people are doing, how they are appropriating this territory, or imagine how a person might occupy your design proposal.

3

Begin from the inside out. Write from the first-person voice ("I"), and in the present tense. Either be yourself – literally yourself as a user of the space you are analysing or designing, or become another – writing the "I" from the point of view of a person of a different age or gender or background. Write what the "I" of your text sees, feels, hears, and experiences directly in the space(s).

4

If you need a starting point, start by describing what the body is actually doing – "I am sitting..." Begin small and close-up. What way is the light falling? What surface is the hand touching? And so on. Then move outwards from your body. In building your writing, think of what comprises an effective 1:50 representation: spatial character, light, texture, atmosphere. Write this as inhabited, by the "I" of the piece, and from there, by others.

5

Read your text(s) out loud. Listen to how they sound. Consider how these first drafts might be shaped into a larger piece of writing, perhaps with an overall narrative, or perhaps as stand-alone episodes. There is no right or wrong here. You are exploring spatial writing, exploring writing as a design tool. You might find this approach to writing helpful as a way of sketching an idea, as a way of getting stuck into a space that you have been avoiding drawing in detail, or as a way of considering the space(s) of your analysis or design work from alternative perspectives. The options are numerous.

assignment

colophon

REPOSITORY
49 Methods and Assignments for Writing Urban Places

Authors
Blagoja Bajkovski
Jesus Balado Frias
Onorina Botezat
Jens Brandt
Yasmin M. Crespo Claudio
Alina Cristea
Serap Durmus Ozturk
Mirian Estela Nogueira Tavares
Emilio Gallardo
Juan García Esparza
Dragoș Gherghescu
Indre Grazuleviciute-Vileniske
Bogdan Guiu
Klaske Havik
Jeremy Allan Hawkins
Menatulla Hendawy
Konstantinos Ioannidis
Francisco J. Escobar Borrego
Laura Jankauskaite-Jureviciene
Alasdair Jones
Filip Jovanovski
Hanna Kahrola
Vilma Karvelyte-Balbieriene
Kinga Kimic
Panu Lehtovuori
Mattias Malk
Charlotte von Meijenfeldt
Maarten Meijer
Marija Mano Velevska
Jorge Mejía Hernández
Dalia Milián Bernal
Lorin Niculae
Eleni Oureilidou
Fernando P. Ferreira
Luc Pauwels
Alexandra Purnichescu
Ana Rafailovska
Jane Rendell
Esteban Restrepo Restrepo
Sophie van Riel
Omayra Rivera Crespo
Anna Ryan Moloney
Rossella Salerno
Luis Santiago Baptista
Irmaris Santiago Rodríguez
Clara Sarmento
Irina Scobiola
Marichela Sepe
Aleksandar Staničić
Quintel Eileen Stornebrink
Heidi Svennigsen Kajita
Mattia Thibault
Ivana Vaseva
Slobodan Velevski
Jurga Vitkuviene
Willie Vogel
Italo de Vroom
Juliana Wexel
Caendia Wijnbelt
Saskia de Wit
Kestutis Zaleckis

Editors
Carlos Machado e Moura
Dalia Milián Bernal
Esteban Restrepo Restrepo
Klaske Havik
Lorin Niculae

English proofreading
Christopher Clarkson

Graphic design
Studio Sanne Dijkstra

Publisher
nai010 Publishers, Rotterdam

Acknowledgement

This publication is based upon work from COST Action CA18126 Writing Urban Places, supported by COST (European Cooperation in Science and Technology). COST is a funding agency for research and innovation networks. Our Actions help connect research initiatives across Europe and enable scientists to grow their ideas by sharing them with their peers. This boosts their research, career and innovation.

COST Action Writing Urban Places core team

Klaske Havik
Susana Oliveira
Jorge Mejía Hernández
Onorina Botezat
Sonja Novak
Angeliki Sioli
Giuseppe Resta

Carlos Machado e Moura
Dalia Milián Bernal
Slobodan Velevski
Luis Santiago Baptista
Kinga Kimic
Marcel Pikhart

Weblink
www.cost.eu
www.writingurbanplaces.eu

isbn 9789462087798

© 2023 the authors, nai010 publishers, Rotterdam

All rights reserved. No part of this publication may be reproduced, stored in a retrieval system, or transmitted in any form or by any means, electronic, mechanical, photocopying, recording or otherwise, without the prior written permission of the publisher. For works of visual artists affiliated with a CISAC-organization the copyrights have been settled with Pictoright in Amsterdam. © 2023, c/o Pictoright Amsterdam

This publication is supported by:

**COST Action CA18126 Writing Urban Places:
New Narratives of the European City**

Writing Urban Places proposes an innovative investigation and implementation of a process for developing human understanding of communities, their society, and their situatedness. By recognising the value of local urban narratives – stories rich in information regarding citizens socio-spatial practices, perceptions and expectations – the Action aims to articulate a set of concrete literary devices within a host of spatial disciplines; bringing together scientific research in the fields of literary studies, urban planning and architecture; and positioning this knowledge vis-à-vis progressive redevelopment policies carried out in medium-sized cities in Europe.

Working Group 3, focusing on methodology, is lead by Carlos Machado e Moura and Dalia Milián Bernal. This working group is dedicated to the articulation of methods to unveil, study, and write urban narratives and to explore their potential for strategies of design, to generate new (and counter) narratives, and to reveal subjugated voices.

writinG urban places